An Illustrated Business Dictionary
for Europe

Acknowledgements
The author wishes to thank the following for assistance and permission to
reproduce material, but any errors or omissions are the responsibility of the author.

British Telecom
Central Office of Information
Peggy Clifford
European Commission
K.J. Lowering & Co Ltd
Lloyds Bank plc
Midland Bank plc
National Consumer Council
Royal Mail
Soft Studies
The Stock Exchange
TSB Bank

An Illustrated
Business Dictionary
for Europe

ALAN WHITCOMB
BA, MEd, PhD

STANLEY THORNES (PUBLISHERS) LTD

First published in 1992 by:
Stanley Thornes (Publishers) Ltd
Old Station Drive
Leckhampton
CHELTENHAM GL53 0DN

ISBN 0-7487–1361-1

British Library Cataloguing in Publication Data
Whitcomb, Alan
  An illustrated business dictionary.
  I. Title
  658.4

ISBN 0-7487-1361-1

Typeset by Cambridge Composing (UK) Ltd
Printed and bound in Great Britain at The Bath Press, Avon

ABC Guides Railway, airways and shipping guides which are published monthly providing details of schedules, fares, etc.

A–Z Street Guides Detailed street maps of major towns. Which show the numbering direction of buildings in each street as well as giving details of places of public interest.

Abbreviations The following are the main abbreviations that are commonly used in business.

General

∵	because	enc(s).	enclosure(s)
∴	therefore	i.e.	that is
&	and	inst.	instant, current month
@	at	Ltd	limited liability
%	per cent, per hundred	memo	memorandum
c/o	care of	p.a.	per annum, each year
Co.	company	PLC	public limited company
dept.	department	re. ref.	reference to
ditto, do	the same	VDU	visual display unit
e.g.	for example		

Trading

a.s.a.p.	as soon as possible	ex works	price at seller's premises
c.f.	cost and freight	f.o.b.	free on board (ship)
c.i.f.	cost, insurance and freight	f.o.c.	free of charge
		f.o.r.	free on rail
COD	cash on delivery	p.p.	pages, per pro (on behalf
CWO	cash with order		of)
E & O E	errors and omissions excepted	P.P.	parcel post

Accounts

a/c	account	c/f	carried forward
c/d	carried down	Cr.	creditor
bal	balance	Dr.	debtor
b/d	brought down	PAYE	Pay As You Earn
b/f	brought forward	SAYE	Save As you Earn

These are some of the most used business abbreviations.

Above Par Higher than nominal value. It is a term used in relation to shares and other forms of security. The nominal value is the face value on the share. (See also Below Par)

ACAS (Advisory Conciliation and Arbitration Service) A government-funded group available for use by both employers and employees to try to find a solution to an industrial dispute that is acceptable to both sides. ACAS offers advice to employers and unions to try to improve industrial relations.

Acceptance   Where the drawee of a bill of exchange writes on the bill that they have accepted the document by signing and usually making it payable at their bank on sight or on a determinable date. (Refer also Bill of Exchange and Acceptor)

Accepting House   A merchant bank which specialises in accepting or guaranteeing payment of bills of exchange. The fact that the bank has countersigned the bill increases its trustworthiness; 'accepting' the bill in this way makes the bank liable to pay the amount outstanding if the original person fails to pay when due to do so.

Acceptor   A person who accepts liability by promising to pay a debt on a bill of exchange should the original signatory default. Acceptance of liability is signified by signing across the front of the bill.

Access   A credit card system run jointly by the major UK clearing banks, with the exception of Barclays, to provide personal credit and a convenient method of paying for purchases by the cardholder.

Accident Book   A record of all industrial accidents that must be kept by all firms over a certain size in the UK.

Accident Insurance   Types of insurance other than fire, marine and life which are categorised under accident insurance, for example, motor, personal accident, theft, liability and contractors' insurance, etc.

Account   1) A term used in business to refer to an amount of money owed by a person or organisation to another. The term is also used as reference to goods sold on credit (on account).   2) The principal divisions of The Stock Exchange calendar. An account usually runs for two weeks. Debts are normally paid at the end of an account.

Accountant   A person who has responsibility for the keeping and recording of accounts. Usually such a person will have professional qualifications such as Chartered Status.

Accounting   The classification, recording, and interpretation of financial transactions periodically so that statements can be prepared to indicate a summary of these transactions or the financial condition of the business.

Account Day   The day on which all bargains entered into by Members of The Stock Exchange are settled.

Account Payee Only   The wording added to the crossing of a cheque to instruct the bank to pay the money only into the account of the payee named on the cheque, and the cheque cannot be cashed immediately

Accounts Department   The department of a firm responsible for monitoring all payments in and out of the business, and maintenance of cash flow. It may also be responsible for wage payments. It is sometimes called the Finance Department.

Accrued   An amount of money that is outstanding or due to be paid by a specified date.

Accumulated   A situation where money has built up through profits over a period of time for a particular purpose such as purchase of assets.

Achievement   A feeling of success at doing something well. This is an important factor in motivating people to work hard and effectively.

Acid Test   An accounting term which refers to the ratio of the total cash, trade, and marketable securities of a business to its current liabilities i.e. a measure of a firm's liquidity and its ability to meet its short-term debts. A desirable ratio would generally not be less than 1.1 (or 110 per cent), but it may well be that some firms are able to operate safely at a much lower level.

Acknowledgement of Order   Sent from seller to buyer it confirms receipt of official order and willingness to supply.

Acteur   Amélioration des Conditions de Travail en Europe. A forum for national institutions for the improvement of working conditions. It was set up by the European Foundation for the Improvement of Living and Working Conditions.

Active Partner   A partner who is active in the management of a partnership, and has unlimited liability, that is, such a partner is fully liable for the debts of the business.

Act of God   An insurance term sometimes used to refer to occurrences that could not reasonably have been foreseen such as, storm, lightning, flood, etc.

Actuary   A statistician who calculates insurance premium based on the degree of risk involved.

ADC Telephone Call (Advice of Duration and Charge)   An operator-connected telephone call timed by the operator who advises the caller length of call and charge incurred. A fee is charged for this service.

Adjournment   Usually with the approval of those present, the chairperson may discontinue or suspend a meeting to be continued at another time.

Adjuster   An independent person who assesses an insurance claim, and adjusts the compensation for the loss fairly between the insurance company and its policyholder.

Ad Valorem   The Latin for according to value. It is generally used in connection with taxes which are levied according to the value, i.e., a percentage of the value of the item or service being sold.

Advance   A term sometimes used for a short-term loan or some other form of credit made available on the understanding that it will be paid back at a later date. It is often used when someone is expecting payment from a third party; for example, a bank may advance money to a builder to build a house who repays it once she or he has sold the house.

Advertising   A commercial activity which assists trade by making potential customers aware of the goods or services a firm has to offer through the publication or broadcasting of information, usually with the aim of stimulating sales. The most commonly used channels through which sellers can advertise to the public are posters hoardings, direct mailings, brochures, leaflets, cinema, television, radio, newspapers, and magazines.

- **Campaign** – A programme of activities designed to stimulate awareness of a company's goods or services.
- **Standards Authority** – A body which investigates complaints against advertisements. It also administers codes of advertising practice which are a set of rules to which advertisers and advertisements should conform.

Advice Note   A trading document sent from a seller to a buyer to inform them that goods ordered have been despatched.

Advice of Shipment A document sent by an exporter to an importer, telling them the goods have been dispatched and giving the dispatch details.

Aids to Trade Those services which help traders in their distribution of goods, for example, insurance, banking, advertising, transport, communications, etc.

After-hours Dealings Dealings done after the official close of The Stock Exchange which count as the first deals done for the following business day. Also known as 'early bargains'.

After-sales Service A repair and maintenance service provided by a retailer or manufacturer on goods sold.

Agenda A list of items to be discussed at a meeting. The agenda is usually circulated to members prior to the meeting. The items on an agenda are listed in a generally accepted way.

AGENDA

1 **Apologies** received (usually in letter form) from those unable to be at the meeting.
2 **Minutes** the minutes or notes made from the last meeting are read.
3 **Matters arising** (out of the minutes) discussion and follow-up of matters or decisions taken at the last meeting.
4 **Correspondence** discussion of important letters received since the last meeting.
5 **Reports** may be made by people who have special information to give to the meeting, for example, reporting back from the work of a committee.
6 **Special matters** here will be discussed the purpose of the present meeting; decisions which have to be made; proposals to be discussed and noted on; action to be followed before the next meeting.
7 **Next meeting** date, time and place of next meeting.
8 **Any other business (AOB)** at this point members bring up matters or questions not included in the agenda.

An agenda follows an accepted form of order in presentation.

Agent   A person authorised or delegated to act on behalf of another in a business transaction, for example, an insurance company which is authorised to make contracts on behalf of a client.

Agent Wholesaler   A wholesale trader who buys and sells goods on behalf of his or her customers. They provide the service of finding buyers for sellers, or finding sellers for buyers.

Agra-Europe   An independent weekly news service on European and world developments affecting the production and marketing of food and agricultural products. It is particularly noted for its in-depth reports about EC Common Agricultural Policy matters.

Agri-monetary System   A term which refers to the 'green currency system' and Monetary Compensatory Amounts operated by the EC under the Common Agricultural Policy. The system has the effect of preventing a common market in agricultural produce.

Air Freight Market   A central market where cargo space for air freight can be negotiated. In the UK it is located in the Baltic Exchange.

Air Mail   A service provided by the Post Office in the UK which sends letters and parcels by aeroplane to destinations abroad.

Air Waybill   A document used in air transport as a receipt given to the consignor (the sender) by the airline. It is the airfreight equivalent of the Bill of Lading used in shipping.

Alarm Call   An arrangement whereby a telephone company operator will ring a particular telephone number at a certain time. This service can also be programmed automatically on System X exchanges.

Alien   Foreign born resident who is not naturalised

Allotment Letter   A document from a company informing someone that they have been allotted new shares. This letter is of value and may act as a temporary or permanent Share Certificate.

Allowance   A reduction in the liability to pay a debt, for example, allowance against tax liability.

Alpha Stocks   One of the four categories of securities quoted on The Stock Exchange through the Stock Exchange Automated Quotation System (SEAQ). Alpha stocks are those most actively traded.

Altener   A European Commission programme for the development of alternative energy sources.

Amalgamation (or Merger) The joining together of two or more businesses into one organisation, although they may retain different names under a unified structure for marketing purposes.

Ambassador A representative of a foreign country whose function is to look after the interests of the nationals of their home country while abroad and to keep their home country informed of information of political and trade importance.

Amendment A proposal to alter a motion put forward to a meeting by adding or deleting words. The term can also refer to an alteration to a document.

Annual General Meeting (AGM) A meeting open to all members of an organisation. Used for election of principal officers (chairperson, secretary and treasurer) and for officers and committee members to make reports and summaries to all members. It is held once a year. Companies must hold an AGM.

Annual Percentage Rate (APR) The true rate of interest charged for credit.

Annual Report Any type of financial statement or summary facility prepared at yearly intervals. Company directors are legally obliged to produce an annual report.

Annuity Fixed sums of money paid at regular intervals to someone who has a fully paid-up life assurance policy.

Annuitant A person who invests a sum of money with an insurance company which guarantees regular periodic payments for a fixed period or for the rest of the life of the annuitant. This type of policy is known as an annuity.

Ante-dated Cheque A back-dated cheque. Ante-dating has the effect of shortening the life of the cheque, which becomes stale six months from the date written on it.

Apollo The joint project of the European Commission and the European Space Agency for satelite and digital communication.

Application Form An official form used by the public to apply direct for shares offered by a public company. This form is printed as part of the prospectus. The term can also be applied to forms for application for employment.

Appraisal An assessment or estimation of the worth, value, or quality of a person or thing.

Appreciation The increase in value of property. (See Depreciation)

Apprenticeship The time spent by a trainee (or apprentice) in a company learning a skill by working with skilled employees. Sometimes such a position will also involve part-time study.

Approximation An EC term that refers to the process of reaching agreement on measures which make the national laws of the various Member States more similar.

Aptitude Test A specially devised test used to assess the suitability of someone to do a particular job.

Arbitrage The purchase of currencies, securities, or commodities in one market for immediate resale in others in order to profit from unequal prices.

Arbitration Where both sides in an industrial dispute request that the dispute goes before an arbitrator (an umpire). Both sides agree to accept the verdict of the arbiter.

Arbitrator An independent middleman who is called upon by two parties, for example, the insured and the insurer, to settle a disagreement. After each side presents its argument, the arbitrator will pass judgement and it must be accepted by both sides.

Arbitrator's Clause A clause in an insurance policy which provides for the appointment of an arbitrator should the insurer and the insured come to disagreement over the indemnity.

Arrears A sum that is unpaid or overdue for payment.

Articled Clerk A commercial apprentice working in a business or professional office for a nominal salary until they have passed qualifying professional examinations.

Articles of Association A document which has to be completed during the formation of a company and submitted to the Registrar of Companies. It outlines the internal relationship of the business, i.e. the broad way in which the internal organisation will operate. Articles of Association contain:

- The rights of shareholders
- Method of election of directors
- Division of profits
- Manner in which meetings are to be conducted.

Assay An assessment of the quality and value of precious metals in accordance with standards laid down by the UK Parliament.

Assembly A method of production whereby units are built on an assembly line until the finished article is complete.

Assets The various kinds of property of value owned by a business. Assets can be divided into two groups:

- **Fixed assets** – durable (long term) items which are used over a long period of time and are tied up in permanent use, for example, buildings, machinery, furniture, vehicles.
- **Current assets** – items which are continually changing in quantity, or total value or nature, for example, stocks, cash, bankbalance and money owed to the business by its customers (debtors)

Asset Stripping The purchase of a firm at less than its true value for the purpose of selling its assets at a profit with the objective of closing the firm down.

Assisted Areas Parts of the UK with high levels of unemployment where businesses are given grants and other aid by the Government to encourage them to set up a new factory or office.

Association of European Airlines (AEA) A trade association of the international airlines of western Europe.

Assurance (See Life Assurance)

At Best A condition to deal 'at the lowest possible price' in the case of a buying order, and 'at the highest possible price' in the case of a selling order. It is used in relation to instructions given to an agent to buy or sell shares on behalf of someone.

At Call A term used, usually in reference to the money market, indicating money that is repayable on demand.

Attorney An alternative name for a lawyer or solicitor. A person legally appointed by another to act on their behalf as agent.

Atypical Workers Workers such as home-workers, part-time employees, and people who work from their homes.

Auction   A market situation where buyers or their agents bid for the purchase of items. Sometimes the items for sale are shown by a representative sample. The purchase goes to the highest bidder.

Audit   An examination of business accounts by an independent auditor, usually carried out annually.

Auditor   A person who examines the accounts of a business. This may be an employee of the firm (internal audit) or someone from outside the organisation (external audit).

Austerity   A period of slack in business operations, and often influencing high unemployment.

Authority   The permission given for one person to act on behalf of another.

Automation   A method of production using machinery to perform tasks formerly carried out by humans.

Average Clause   A clause in an insurance policy which protects an insurer against under-insurance by stating that, if a partial loss occurs, the amount payable will be proportional to the ratio of the amount covered by the insurance to the actual value of the risk.

Average Cost   The average cost per unit of production. The total cost is the cost of producing all output over a given period of time. For example, if the total cost of producing 100 chairs is £1500 the average cost would be £15.

Average Revenue   The revenue received per unit sold. It is the average price received for a product.

Average Stock   The value of average stock. This is calculated by adding the stock value at the beginning and at the end of the trading period and dividing by two. For example,

Stock value at beginning of year	£40,000
Stock value at the end of year	£60,000
	£100,000

$$\text{Average stock value} \quad = \quad \frac{£100,000}{2} \quad = \quad £50,000$$

Backwardation A Stock Exchange term which refers to the charge paid by a seller who wishes to delay delivery of some shares to a buyer until a later date.

Bad Debt The money which is owed to a business by customers or debtors but which will never be paid back.

Balance The difference between the debit and credit sides of an account, for example, the amount held in a bank account at any particular time.

- **of payments** – A statement of the difference in total value of all payments made to other countries and the total payment received from them.This balance includes both visible and invisible trade.
  a) A favourable balance of payments is when there is a net inflow of capital.
  b) An adverse balance is when there is a net currency outflow.
- **of trade** – This refers to the difference between the value of goods a country imports and the value of goods exported. Because the goods can be seen they are collectively called 'visibles'.
  a) When exports exceed imports the balance is said to be favourable because a surplus has been created.
  b) When imports exceed exports the trade gap is said to be adverse because a deficit has been created.
- **sheet** – A statement showing the financial position of a company at a particular moment in time. It is basically two lists, one showing all sorts of property (assets) the business owns, and one which shows the items for which the business is liable (liabilities).

BalanceSheet **Soft Studies plc** as at 31 December 199__

Liabilities	£	Assets	£
Capital	100 000	Fixed Assets	
Long-term liabilities		Land and buildings	80 000
Mortgage	40 000	Equipment/Fittings	20 000
		Vehicles	10 000
Current liabilities		Current assets	
		Stock*	32 000
Tax to be paid	2 400	Debtors	12 000
Bank overdraft	5 600	Bank balance	5 400
Creditors	8 000	Cash float	600
	£160 000		£160 000

*at cost price

A firm's balance sheet shows where the capital used in a business has come from, and what it has been spent on. It shows the financial position of the company at any particular moment in time. It is basically two lists, one showing all sorts of property the company owns (assets) and one which shows who the company is responsible to for various sums of money (liabilities). The assets are placed in order of 'liquidity', the most liquid (easiest or quicket to turn into cash) being at the bottom.

Ballot   A method of voting. With a secret ballot votes are marked on a slip of paper by voters and then put in a ballot box for later counting. A postal ballot avoids the need for voters to actually meet.

Baltic Exchange   A world market centre for shipping and air chartering which is situated in the City of London. It contains the following important markets:

- Freight market
- Air freight market
- Grain futures market
- Oil and oilseeds market

Bank   An institution which as acts a link between borrowers and lenders, accepts deposits and provides facilities for transferring deposits

by cheque. Banks make a profit by charging borrowers a higher rate of interest than that paid to depositors.

- **Bankers'** – A term sometimes used when referring to The Bank of England. All the banks have accounts with the it, and, during the process of cheque clearing, debits and credits are made to these accounts as a means of interbank settlement.
- **Cards** – A number of cards that can be used in association with bank accounts. The most important of which are the cash dispenser card, the cheque card, and the credit card. Each of these is explained at the appropriate point in this book.
- **Charges** – The amount debited to a customer's account by a bank which represents the fee for running the account. Charges are usually only applied if the agreed credit balance is not maintained.
- **Draft** – A cheque drawn on a bank instead of an individual account. A bank draft is as good as cash because it is guaranteed by the bank. The bank is happy to guarantee the draft because the customer either

pays the value (plus a fee) of the draft in advance, or they put up something of value as collateral (security).

- **Giro** – A circulating banking system which makes transfer of funds directly (credit transfer) into a particular bank account, irrespective of which bank the account is held with. There are two basic methods of credit transfer:

    1) Single transfer: a form is filled in to make a payment directly into a stated bank account.

    2) Multiple transfer: the payee writes out a single cheque payable to their own bank for an amount to cover payments to several different people (for example, wages of all employees). A schedule or list is given to the bank showing details of the several bank accounts to which payments should be made.

- **Giro credit** – A form used to pay money into a bank account.
- **Loan** – An advance made by a bank to be repaid by the borrower over an agreed period of time. The total amount of the loan is transferred to the borrower's account and the customer is required to pay interest on the total amount borrowed, even if they do not use all of the loan immediately. The loan is repaid in regular fixed amounts, including interest, over a period of time agreed between the bank and the borrower.
- **Overdraft** – A current account holder is allowed to write out cheques for more money that they have in their account with the permission of the bank When this happens the account is said to be 'in the red'. The actual amount the account is overdrawn is known as the overdraft. Interest is calculated daily on the amount the account is overdrawn.

Bank, Central (See Central Bank)

Bank Clearing (See Clearing House)

Bankers' Order   An order from a bank customer requesting that periodic payments are made on their behalf, for example, by standing order

Bank of England   The bank which serves as the UK central bank. It is also known as the 'The Bank' or 'The Old Lady of Threadneedle Street' It was nationalised in 1946. It has the following functions:

- Banker to the government
- Banker to foreign banks
- Banker to the commercial banks
- Control of issue of bank notes
- Lender of last resort to the money market
- Adviser to the government on monetary policy
- Supervisor of the financial community. (See also Central Bank)

Bank, Merchant   Private firms that offer highly specialised services. These are not banks in the commonly understood sense but are almost exclusively for business customers. They offer services such as:

- Accepting: (lending their name to) a bill of exchange issued by a less well-known trader so that it becomes more acceptable because of the bank's good reputation.
- Issuing: (organising) first issues of new shares for companies.

Bankruptcy   Where a debtor (someone who owes money) is unable to repay debts owed, the creditors (those owed the money) may apply to a Court for a receiving order to be made. If the Court agrees that the order should be made, an official receiver will be appointed to take over the debtor's affairs. If the debts cannot be cleared from the assets available or potential income, the debtor is declared 'bankrupt' and must cease trading.

Barclaycard A credit card system operated by Barclays Bank to provide a source of credit and a convenient method of making payments. It is not confined to Barclays Bank customers. The card also acts as a cheque guarantee card for account holders.

Bar Code A label or sign made up of a pattern of vertical lines of varying thickness. The code formed by the lines can be transmitted to a computer by a light reader device, allowing stock records to be updated and items valued automatically (for example, on a till receipt).

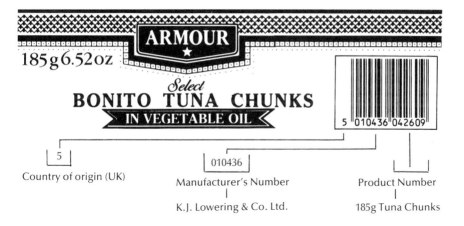

Bargain A term used to describe the agreement to purchase or sell securities on The Stock Exchange. No 'special price' is implied.

Barter The exchange of one thing for another without the use of money. Barter was the earliest method of trading.

Base Rate A rate of interest set by a financial institution to which the interest rates on most of its loans are linked.

Bear Someone who sells shares anticipating a fall in market prices, perhaps intending to buy them back later at a lower price. In a 'bearish' market prices are generally falling.

Bearer Cheque   A cheque in which the payee is not specified. Instead the words 'the bearer' or 'cash' are entered on the cheque.

Below Par   A term used when the market price of stocks, shares and other securities are below their face or nominal value. (See Above Par)

BENELUX   An Economic Union consisting of the countries of Belgium, The Netherlands and Luxembourg.

Berlaymont   The headquarters building of the European Commission in Brussels.

Best Lending Rate   The rate of interest charged by banks to its best customers, i.e., the lowest rate the bank will offer for loans. It is also referred to as prime lending rate.

Big Bang   The nickname for the the change in The Stock Exchange rules and practices started in October 1980, bringing UK practice more into line with that of major Stock Exchanges overseas.

Big Four   The four biggest UK commercial banks; Barclays, Lloyds, Midland and National Westminster.

Bilateral Agreements   The agreements negotiated directly between two countries or two negotiating partners, for example, the USA and China

Bill   A security having a life of one year or less which is sold for less than face value (discounted) in order to encourage people to buy it. It gives the drawee a short period of credit at a relatively low cost. The drawee then repurchases (redeems) it at a specified date at its face value.

Billingsgate   The London wholesale produce market for fish. It was recently resited to new premises in West India Dock Road.

Bill of Exchange   A method of payment where a seller draws up a document and the buyer signs it agreeing to pay an amount due at some future date. The signed bill of exchange can be kept by the seller until payment is made, sold to someone else at a discount (discounted), or used as collateral against a loan (negotiated). The bill of exchange is particularly evident in international trade. (See Discounting)

Having received as 'accepted' bill of exchange back from his customer abroad, the exporter may sell the bill – perhaps to a banker or discount house, at a 'discounted price'. The exporter will now send the goods to his customer and the customer will pay the full value of the bill to the new owner.

Bill of Lading
A document used in the shipping of goods. It shows details of the goods, their destination and the terms under which the shipping company agrees to carry the goods. Three copies are produced.

1) The first is retained by the exporter
2) The second is given to the ship's captain
3) The third is sent to the importer who has to produce his copy to take possession of goods on arrival.

Blank Cheque
A cheque which has been signed but has not had the amount to be paid inserted because the details are not known. The drawer usually allows the payee to fill in the amount to be paid.

Blacking
A form of restrictive practice used in an industrial dispute. Union members may refuse to work on or move certain machines or equipment, or refuse to work with certain other people or groups.

Black-leg
A term of abuse often applied to a person who acts against the interests of a trade union such as by working during a strike or taking over a striker's job. It is also referred to as 'scab'.

Blue Chip
A term used to describe shares with the highest status as investment, particularly in the industrial markets.

Board of Directors   A group of people elected by shareholders (owners of a company) to manage the business. Directors are elected for a set period after which they can stand for re-election.

Bond   A certificate received in exchange for a loan, entitling the holder to be paid interest at a fixed rate. The bond usually also names a date (redemption date) when the holder is entitled to the return of the loan.

Bonded Warehouse   A warehouse in which imported goods can be stored under Customs supervision until the importer is able to pay the import duty due, or until the goods are re-exported.

Bonus   A method of wage payment given to employees as a share of additional profits gained by the employer due to increased effort or efficiency of the work group or individual.

Bounce   The dishonouring of a cheque due to insufficient funds being available.

Brainstorming   A term used to describe a group method of generating creative ideas and thinking.

Branding   The process of giving products a distinctive name to enable the consumer to recognise the product easily. Manufacturers try to create a 'brand image' through advertising resulting in only needing to keep the brand name in the public eye and reducing the need to spend time and money describing the virtues of the product. Large retailers buy products from manufacturers with their 'own brand' displayed on them, for example, St Michael is the brand name of Marks and Spencer.

Break-even   The point at which revenues and costs are exactly equal. When a business is operating at above this point, it usually shows a profit; if it is operating below break-even point, it usually shows a loss. The costs and revenues are used in break-even analysis that can be depicted on a break-even chart. See the illustration on the opposite page.

Bridging Loan   A loan which is provided by a bank as a temporary measure for a very short period (a few days or weeks) until other expected funds become available.

British Standards Institution (BSI)   An organisation which publishes a series of standards intended to ensure that a wide range of consumer products are safe and fit for the purpose they are intended. Products that meet the stringent standards laid down can attach marks of the BSI. The marks of BSI are the kitemark and the safety mark. The

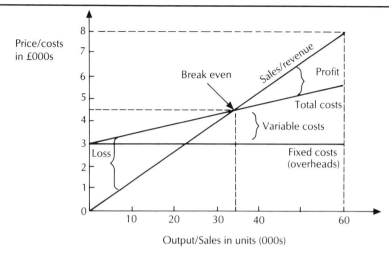

Break-even chart

BSI helps to develop European and international standards through its membership of international organisations with similar aims.

BS 4224

Kitemark   Safety Mark

Broker A person who buys and sells on behalf of others on a commission (brokerage) basis – an intermediary between parties to a business transaction, for example, stockbroker, shipbroker, insurance broker.

Broker/Dealers   Stock Exchange Member Firms which buy or sell shares as agents for investors, or as principals for their own account with other Member Firms or outside investors, or they can act in a dual capacity as both agent and principal. Some Broker/Dealers specialise as Market Makers. (See also Market Makers)

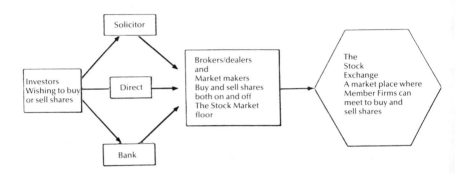

Only Member Firms of The Stock Exchange are allowed to take part in dealing on the Exchange and outsiders must carry out their buying and selling through them.

Broker, Lloyd's   Key figures in the Insurance Market. Underwriters at Lloyd's have no direct contact with the public who are seeking insurance. It is the broking firms who keep in touch with customers all over the world and bring their insurance needs into the central market and obtaining the best possible terms for them. (See also Insurance Market)

Bucket Shop   A nickname applied to businesses which operate outside official market bodies offering cut-price services such as cheap air tickets.

Budget   An estimate of expected income and expenditure over a given period of time, usually based on a systematic plan.

- **Account** – A bank account which helps the account holder to even out annual household expenses. The total value of all the account holder's major annual expenses is divided by 12 to give a monthly average. The account holder agrees to pay the monthly average to the bank, and the bank agrees to meet the payment of all the special budget cheques, even if the account becomes overdrawn. There is a charge for each cheque transfer, but interest is paid whilst the account is in credit and interest is charged when the account is overdrawn.

• **Day** – The day when the Chancellor of the Exchequer presents to parliament the Government's planned expenditure for the year, and the way that it is intended to raise the income required.

Budgetary Control The processes used in business management to try and ensure that the firm remains within the budget predicted for it. (See also Cash Flow)

Bug A mistake or error in a computer program.

Building Society An organisation which aims to operate to the mutual benefit of the small saver and people who wish to borrow money to buy their own homes.

Bulletin of the European Communities An official report published 11 times a year on the activities of the European Commission and other EC institutions.

Bulk Carrier A purpose-built ship designed to carry specific bulk cargo such as ore and grain.

Bull A Stock Exchange speculator who buys or holds shares anticipating a price rise and hoping to make a profit by selling at a higher price. In a 'bullish' market prices are generally rising.

Bureaucracy Administration system in a large organisation. It is sometimes the source of 'red tape' which slows down decision-making process.

Bureau de Change A place where currency can be exchanged for a fee.

Bureaufax The name of the British Telecom facsimile transmission service (see also Facsimile Transmission)

Business

• **Card (calling card)** – A card presented by business callers to give their name, name and address of their company and the position they hold.

```
THE ALDEN PRESS
───────────────────────────
ALDEN PRESS LIMITED
OSNEY MEAD · OXFORD · OX2 0EF
Tel 0865 249071   Telex 83636 ALPRES G   Fax 0865 249070



LINDA SPOONER
Sales Executive
```

A business card gives useful information about the presenter and saves a lot of questions.

- **Cycle** – Another name for trade cycle; the tendency of fluctuations between boom and depression in industrial and commercial activity over a period of years.
- **Interruption insurance** – A form if insurance which provides compensation against loss of business as a result of fire or some other damage preventing the business from operating in its normal manner. It is also known as consequential loss insurance.
- **Names** – Where individuals trade under a name different from that of the owners they are using a business name.
- **Reply service** – A postal service in the UK. A trader provides potential customers with specially printed envelopes displaying a licence number and the class of postage. The trader is charged with the cost of postage by the Post Office on all letters received, thus encouraging custom. In order to use this facility a licence must be obtained from the Head Postmaster, for which an annual fee is payable.
- **Unit** – An organisation engaged in business. The type of unit is determined by identifying who provided the capital and who receives the profits. Businesses in the public sector (state-owned) are organised as public corporations. There are a number of different types of organisation in the private sector. They are: sole proprietors; partnerships; private limited companies; public limited companies; co-operative societies.

Buyer's Market   A situation where there are more sellers than buyers making it more likely that buyers will secure bargains.

Cabotage The practice of governments reserving the right to transport goods within their territories to their own national companies. In the EC it has the opposite meaning. In other words, in Europe it refers to the right of transporters to be able to carry goods and people inside the territories of other European countries.

Call Rate A banking term that refers to the rate of interest applicable to deposits repayable on demand and not subject to notice.

CAP (See Common Agricultural Policy)

Capital Capital is the money, or the assets bought with money, used to run a business. There are three main sources of capital used in a business:

1) **Share capital** – money subscribed to the company by shareholders. This does not have to be repaid sometime.
2) **Loan capital** – usually a long-term loan to be repaid at sometime
3) **Reserves** – a percentage of gross profits ploughed back into the business.

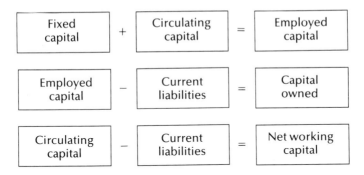

Capital can be usefully divided into the following categories:

- **Fixed capital** – durable assets of a business which are used over a long period of time and are tied up in long-term use, for example, land, buildings, machinery, etc.
- **Circulating capital (working capital)** – assets of business which are continually changing in quantity, total value or nature, for example, stocks, cash, bank balance, money owed by customers.
- **Employed capital** – the total value of all the assets being used by a business i.e. fixed assets plus current assets, but excluding any debts

which are owed by the firm. Debts are not included because they cannot be used to finance the firm's operations until they are received.

- **Capital owned** – net value of the assets actually owned by a business i.e. employed capital minus current liabilities. Current liabilities refers to debts which will have to be repaid in the near future, for example, bank overdraft, debts owed to suppliers, taxes payable to the government.
- **Liquid capital** – that part of current assets which are cash or are easily turned into cash, for example, cash in tills, bank balance, money owed by customers.
- **Net working capital** – current assets minus current liabilities.

Capital, Authorised   The capital of a company as authorised in its memorandum of association. It is sometimes refered to as 'registered' or 'nominal' capital.

Capital Gains Tax   A tax based upon the excess of the proceeds of disposal of a person's assets over their cost. If you buy an asset (e.g. shares) at one price and sell them at another the difference (after allowing for expenses) is your Capital Gain (or Loss). You become liable to Capital Gains Tax when you sell the asset. You only pay the tax if your total Capital Gains (less Losses) in any one year exceed a figure set by the government (it changes from time to time in the Budget).

Capital Gearing   The ratio of fixed interest loans to total capital.

Capital Goods   Fixed assets with long life and which are used to produce goods.

Capital Intensive   A production process that uses a high proportion of capital (usually in the form of machinery) to labour in its operation.

Capitalisation Issue   An issue of shares which results from a company transferring money from its reserves to its permanent capital. These new shares are then distributed to the existing shareholders, in proportion to their existing holdings. It is also known as Free, Bonus or Scrip issue.

Capitalism   An economic system based on the private ownership of the means of production, distribution, and exchange. Such a system is characterised by the freedom of capitalists to operate or manage their property for profit in competitive conditions. Also referred to as 'private enterprise' or 'free enterprise'.

Capital Transfer Tax   A tax which applies to gifts in excess of a certain value made during the lifetime of the donor or at death. Different rates apply to lifetime and death gifts and the liability arises at the time the property is transferred.

Capital Market   A term used to refer to a large number of financial institutions providing long-term loans and the firms seeking them throughout Europe. It is almost entirely confined to business and industry. The following are examples of the lending institutions:

- Insurance companies
- Building societies
- Investment trusts
- Unit trusts
- Pension funds
- Issuing houses (Merchant Banks)
- The Stock Exchange

Carriage Forward   The price of goods including packaging but not including transport costs.

Carriage Paid   The price of goods including packaging and delivery costs.

Carrier   A firm which specialises in transporting goods.

Cartel   A group of separate businesses which have agreed to co-operate in order to control competition. Agreements made are usually directed towards price or output control by establishing market quotas and divisions of territory. A cartel can also be formed by a group of countries with the aim of regulating production and price, for example, OPEC, the oil producing states' cartel.

Cash   The most liquid (easily usable) asset held by a business, either in tills and cash float or in the bank. The term also applies to any instrument of payment that a payee can convert easily and quickly to their own use without incurring a charge.

Cash and Carry   A form of wholesaling whereby the retailer collects purchases himself and pays for them immediately as he leaves the warehouse. The costs saved by eliminating credit and delivery facilities enables the wholesaler to give the retailer lower prices.

Cash and Wrap   A term used in some forms of retailing where payment points are sited around the store and purchases are wrapped for the customer. This eliminates queues near entrances and exits and the packing indicates that the customer has paid for goods they are leaving the store with.

Cash

- **Card** – A card issued to bank customers to enable them to obtain cash from a cash dispenser.
- **Discount** – A discount offered to a buyer by the seller to encourage prompt payment.
- **Dispenser** – A machine set in the wall of a bank and connected to the bank computer. The user feeds a special card into the machine and keys in a personal identity number (PIN). The machine will then issue a sum of money and immediately deduct the amount from the customer's account.
- **Flow** – The flow of money in and out of a business It is the difference between the receipts from sales and the amount spent on expenses such as raw materials, wages, interest paid on loans, dividends paid to shareholders, etc. A trading surplus adds to the reserves whereas a deficit reduces reserves. If you refer to the cash flow diagram it will be obvious that if income from sales is equal to expenditure the firm will not have a cash flow problem. Where expenses exceed income the business may have to obtain additional capital in order to continue operating and avoid bankruptcy. To achieve cash flow is no simple matter. It is important to recognise that payments for goods or services will often not be received until some time after supply. This will mean that the business must budget with this possibility in mind. If the company budgeting is unsound the firm will have to request extended credit from its own suppliers, seek financial support from a bank or some other financial institution, or obtain further capital from another source. This would incur costs from interest payments.

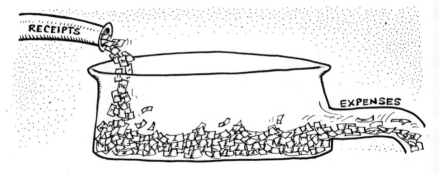

• **Flow statement** – A report of the income and expenditure of an enterprise over a particular period of time, usually one year. The items are listed in the same manner as they might appear on a balance sheet.

Cash on Delivery (COD) An arrangement whereby the carrier of goods will collect payment for the goods before handing them over.

Casting Vote An additional vote sometimes allowed the chairperson of a meeting to enable a decision to be taken when votes are evenly divided between two sides.

Catch Phrase A phrase that becomes popular and is often repeated. Advertisers sometimes use such phrases in their advertisements to try to encourage people to remember their name and their products.

Caveat Emptor The Latin for 'let the buyer beware'. This was the attitude towards the consumer prior to the introduction of the many forms of consumer protection that exist today. The consumer was expected to protect themselves by buying with caution.

CE Communauté Européene – the European Community. When a product displays the CE mark the manufacturer is claiming that it conforms to the requirements of EC legislation.

CEDEFOP The European Centre for the Development of Vocational and Training. The centre is sited in Berlin and it provides a research and discussion forum involving governments, the European Commission, industry, and trade unions. CEDEFOP examines aspects such as training, equal opportunities, youth and migrant workers. It also helps to establish agreements between EC Member States on the acceptance of each others' vocational qualifications.

CEEFAX The BBC information service. CEEFAX and the IBA's version, ORACLE, are known together as TELETEXT.

CELEX The European Community database for information on Community legislation and documentation. CELEX is part of the European Information Service of the European Network for Scientific and Technical Information (EURONET).

CEN Comité Européen de Normalisation – the European Standards organisation based in Brussels which develops, through its member organisations such as the British Standards Institution, European standards for goods.

CENELEC   Comité Européen de Normalisation Electrotechnique – the organisation which develops European standards for electrical goods.

Census   An official count of a population including information such as sex, age, occupation, etc. At the time of carrying out a census the Government take the opportunity to obtain data that would be unlikely to be obtained through other surveys.

Central Bank   A bank nominated by the government to issue bank notes, control credit and to supervise the financial community. Most developed countries have a central bank and in the UK this function is performed by the Bank of England. Other Central Banks of Europe include:

- Belgium – Banque Nationale de Belgique
- Denmark – Danmarks Nationalbank
- France – Banque de France
- Germany – Deutsche Bundesbank
- Greece – Bank of Greece
- Holland – De Nederlandsche Bank
- Italy – Banca d'Italia
- Portugal – Banco de Portugal
- Spain – Banco de Espana

Central Processing Unit   The part of a computer in which the processing of data takes place.

Certificate

- **of experience** – Certificates issued to people by the European Community states confirming that they meet the requirements of the appropriate EC standards and can, therefore, practise in all Member States without having to requalify, for example, occupations such as insurance, hairdressing, etc.
- **of incorporation** – A certificate issued by the Registrar of Companies to a newly-registered company. This certificate gives the company a 'corporate identity' – an identity that is separate from that of the owners.
- **of insurance** – A document providing evidence that insurance has been taken out to cover a named risks, for example, public liability insurance. Employers' Certificate of Liability must displayed on the premises.

- **of motor insurance** – A document confirming motor insurance cover, which by law must be delivered to a policyholder before he can use a vehicle on public roads.
- **of origin** – A document which certifies the country of origin of goods. It is required by an importing country, particularly where it has been agreed that the goods of certain countries will be allowed to enter the country at a more favourable tariff rate than other countries.
- **of posting** – A document issued by the UK Post Office to show that an item has been posted. In addition to the basic Certificate of Posting available for normal mail, the Post Office also issues certificates for special services which provide proof of delivery, for example, Recorded Delivery and Registered Post.

A Recorded Delivery envelope and Certificate of Posting

A Certificate of Posting for a registered packet

Certification   The process which provides or receives proof that a particular product meets certain minimum standards, perhaps checked by some independent body. For example, the British Standards Institution's 'Kitemark' indicates that a product conforms to their stringent standards.

Chain

- **of command** – The path that decisions and orders will follow in an organisation from the top to the bottom of the hierarchy.
- **of distribution** – The process of getting products from the producer to the consumer. The traditional route is usually shown as:

Producer → Wholesaler → Retailer → Consumer

However, the increasing trend of large shops and chains of stores results in the wholesaler sometimes being eliminated from the chain. In addition some goods are supplied direct from the producer to the consumer, thus bypassing both the wholesaler and the retailer.

Chain Store (Multiple Shop)   A group (multiple) of shops spread over an area and linked (chain) under a single name of common ownership. A specialist' chain store sells a narrow range of products (for example, Dewhurst sells meat) whereas a variety chain store sells a range of products (for example, Woolworths, Marks and Spencer, British Home Stores, etc).

Chairperson   A person responsible for the correct conduct of a meeting and summing up of all points discussed. The chairperson can use their casting vote when the meeting is equally divided on a point.

Chambers of Commerce   Organisations composed mainly of local business persons to promote, regulate and protect their interests.

Chancellor of Exchequer   The minister responsible to the Prime Minister for the Treasury. Every year the Chancellor presents the Budget which outlines the Government's income and expenditure plans for the forthcoming year.

Change in Demand   The change in the quantity of a product that consumers are willing and able to buy at different prices.

Channel Tunnel   The tunnel constructed to provide a direct connection between England and France beneath the English Channel.

Charge Cards   Cards issued by some traders to approved customers allowing them to purchase goods on credit. Charge cards are frequently linked to an instalment system operated by the trader, sometimes interest free.

Chartering Agent   A person who represents merchants who wish to charter vessels.

Charter Party   The agreement to hire a ship. Voyage charters cover the hire of a whole ship for a particular voyage. Time charters give the charterer use of the complete vessel for a period of time.

Cheque   A written instruction to a bank (the drawee) to pay money to the account holder (the drawer) or to another person (the payee).

- **card** – A card issued by banks to approved customers. It is used to guarantee payment of a cheque up to the limit stated on the card. Having used the card to guarantee a cheque it is not possible to stop the payment.
- **clearing** – The process of passing a cheque for payment. The appropriate amount is deducted from the drawer's account and passed to the account of the person or company to whom the money is being paid. This is known as the 'clearing system'. Interbank clearing is carried out at the Clearing House where representatives of all the clearing banks meet to settle their debts with each other.

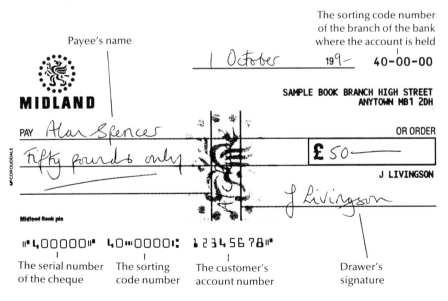

The sorting code number of the branch of the bank where the account is held

Payee's name

| October   19 9 –   40-00-00

SAMPLE BOOK BRANCH HIGH STREET
ANYTOWN MB1 2DH

MIDLAND

PAY   Alan Spencer   OR ORDER

Fifty pounds only   £ 50—

                                         J LIVINGSON

                                         J Livingson

Midland Bank plc

⑆400000⑆ 40⑈0000⑆ 12345678⑈

| The serial number | The sorting | The customer's | Drawer's |
| of the cheque | code number | account number | signature |

Cheque Counterfoil   The stub left in a cheque book when a cheque is torn out. The counterfoil is provided for the personal use of the account holder to provide a record of the way in which the cheque has been used. The counterfoil has no legal significance.

Cheque Crossing   The method of drawing two parallel lines vertically across it. The effect of a cheque crossing is that it must be paid into a bank account; it cannot be exchanged for cash. To turn a crossed cheque into an open cheque the drawer writes 'pay cash' and signs in between the lines of the crossing. Crossed cheques are printed with a 'general' crossing by the bank, but there are a number of set wordings that can be written in between the lines of a crossing to give it 'special' significance.

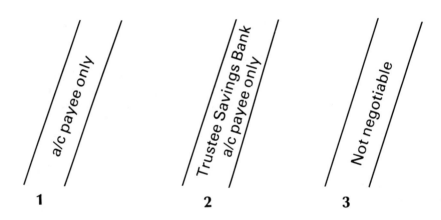

1 *This crossing ensures that the cheque can only be paid into the account of the payee, although they can pay it into their account through any branch they wish.*

2 *This means the same as the above crossing except that the cheque can only be paid in at the branch stated in the crossing.*

3 *When written as a cheque crossing this warns anyone other than the payee accepting the cheque that they do so with some degree of risk. The risk they face is that if the cheque has been stolen or fraudulently used, then the person accepting it is liable to refund the rightful owner with the amount shown on the cheque.*

Cheque, Dishonoured   A cheque which has not been passed for payment by the drawer's bank for some reason. When this happens the cheque is sometimes said to have 'bounced' because it has been returned through the system to the payee. The payee must then find out from the drawer why the cheque has not been passed for payment.

There are several reasons why a cheque might 'bounce'.

- The cheque is post-dated
- The cheque is 'stale' (more than six months old)
- The cheque contains an error
- The signature differs from bank specimen
- The cheque is unsigned
- The drawer has insufficient funds in their account
- The cheque has been altered
- The drawer has instructed the bank not to pass the cheque for payment (the cheque has been 'stopped').

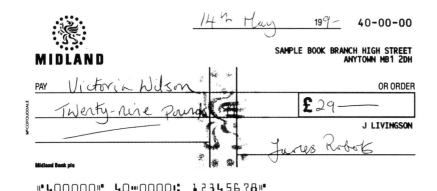

For what reasons do you think a bank would refuse to honour this cheque?

Cheque, Post-dated   A cheque which is dated for some time in the future. The cheque will not be passed for payment until the date shown.

Cheque, Stale   A cheque which has become out of date. The life of a cheque is six months from the date shown on it, after which time it cannot be cashed.

Circulation Slip   A slip of paper attached to a document being circulated to show those people who should read it.

Citizens' Advice Bureaux (CAB)   A voluntary organisation formed to give people advice and to deal with domestic problems such as those related to consumer protection.

Citizen's Europe Advisory Service   A service which gives information on EC citizens' rights under Community law, including free movement and access to benefits which are provided as part of the 'People's Europe' programme.

Claims Assessor   Professionals, either employed by an insurance company or hired by such a company, who specialise in assessing the value of a loss. Their estimation is used as a basis for calculating the indemnity in insurance.

Claims Form   A form which an insured person files with the insurance company to claim the indemnity (amount) due when a loss occurs.

Class Actions   Legal action initiated by one or more people who have decided to combine together to implement action on a particular issue. If successful, the person(s) taking the action (the litigant) would win the argument for others in similar cases against the same defendant. For example, the relative of a person killed in the sinking of a ship, by successfully suing the shipowners, would enable other relatives to obtain compensation without the need for individual action.

Classified Trades Directory (Yellow Pages)   Directories which are issued free of charge to British Telecom telephone subscribers. They list, free of charge, names, addresses and telephone numbers of all business subscribers in alphabetical order by trade. Businesses can pay to have a display or bold face entry.

Clearance Note   A note issued by the Customs authorities stating that the Customs formalities have been completed, which allows the importer to take the goods out of the Customs-controlled area.

Clearing Bank   A bank which is a member of the Clearing House where interbank cheque clearing is carried out daily, e.g. Barclays, Lloyds, Midland and National Westminster.

Clearing House   A place where the clearing banks meet to exchange items and to settle their indebtedness to each other through the accounts they hold with the central bank.

P RAQUEL

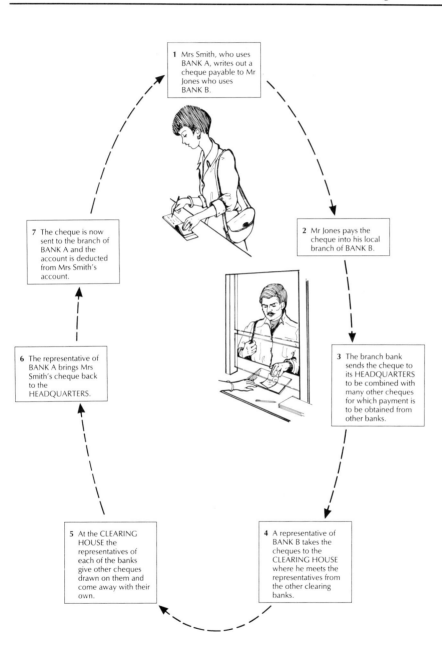

1 Mrs Smith, who uses BANK A, writes out a cheque payable to Mr Jones who uses BANK B.

2 Mr Jones pays the cheque into his local branch of BANK B.

3 The branch bank sends the cheque to its HEADQUARTERS to be combined with many other cheques for which payment is to be obtained from other banks.

4 A representative of BANK B takes the cheques to the CLEARING HOUSE where he meets the representatives from the other clearing banks.

5 At the CLEARING HOUSE the representatives of each of the banks give other cheques drawn on them and come away with their own.

6 The representative of BANK A brings Mrs Smith's cheque back to the HEADQUARTERS.

7 The cheque is now sent to the branch of BANK A and the account is deducted from Mrs Smith's account.

Clearing System   The system of settlement of accounts between dealers where many small items are totalled for convenience of settlement. In banking it refers to the process of passing a cheque from the bank where it is paid in back to the account holder's bank, and ultimately passing payment.

Clerk   The common meaning for someone who works in an office. In some institutions the term has a special meaning. In The Stock Exchange it refers to someone who is employed by a stockbroker either inside or outside the Exchange. Those clerks who work inside can be divided into 'authorised' and 'unauthorised' clerks.

- Authorised clerks have the authority to act on behalf of their principals and to enter into transactions on their behalf.
- Unauthorised clerks are permitted to enter the Exchange but do not have the authority to enter into transactions.

Clock Card/Time Card   A card which employees insert into a time recording device. When an employee is paid by a time rate they may be required to record their arrival and departure at their place of employment. Time of arrival and departure are recorded and the record is used to calculate wage payment due.

Closed Indent Order   An order placed through a broker in which the type of product and the source of supply are specified. Therefore, the broker does not have a choice about where to buy the goods from.

Closed Shop   A restrictive practice whereby the employer agrees to employ only union members.

Coaster   A cargo ship mainly trading around the home coast and usually operating without a timetable.

Codes of Practice   A voluntary form of self-regulation, distinct from legislative control, followed by manufacturers. Many manufacturers belong to 'trade associations' which try to establish codes which all members will follow in order to provide standardised services or products to consumers. For example, manufacturers may agree to certain minimum standards of products, or retailers may agree to a common procedure for dealing with complaints by customers.

Cohesion   A term used particularly in relation to the EC to refer to the policy of ensuring that the least well-off regions of the Community share in Europe's economic growth and do not deteriorate as a region.

This policy is implemented through the use of the regional, social and structural funds.

College of Europe　The College in Bruges, Belgium, providing post-graduate European study programmes in administration, economics and law.

Collateral　A form of guarantee for repayment of a loan of money. It is sometimes referred to as 'secondary' security because the lender will firstly satisfy themselves that the borrower can repay the loan, and secondly may require additional security such as title deeds to property, stocks and shares or other items of value. This is known as collateral.

Collating　The process of collecting pages of a document into some form of sequence. In many offices this is automated.

Collect Calls　A telephone service in which the receiver pays for the call (transfer charge).

Collection Letter　A letter reminding a debtor that he or she still has unsettled debts and asking them to settle them.

Collective Bargaining　A term which refers to the procedures by which wages and conditions of employment are settled through bargaining between the employer and the workers' representatives (for example, trade union) acting on their collective behalf.

COMECON　An association of Communist nations, founded in 1949 to co-ordinate economic development. COMECON includes the countries of Bulgaria, Cuba, Czechoslovakia, Hungary, Mongolia, Poland, Romania, USSR and Vietnam but was disbanded in 1991 and replaced by bilateral agreements.

COMETT　The European Community programme in Education and Training for Technology. It is the EC programme for co-operation between universities and training enterprises in the field of high technology.

Commerce　The name used for the distribution and change of ownership of goods produced. It is also a term sometimes used when referring to tertiary production. It aims to ensure that goods reach the consumer in the right quantity, at the right price at the right time and in the right condition. In order to achieve these aims trade must take place. This can take many forms such as, wholesale, retail, import and export. Trade is assisted by commercial services (aids to trade) banking, finance, insurance, transport and a variety of communications services which include advertising, the post and telecommunication.

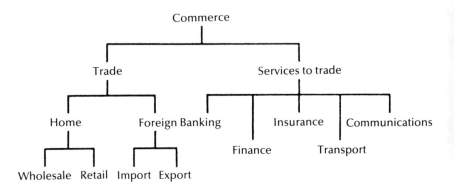

Commercial or Trade Bill   A bill issued by a company.

Commission   A charge usually calculated on a percentage basis and paid or received for a service rendered.

Commission, The   The EC's 'Civil Service', mainly located in Brussels. The Commission is responsible for drafting Community legislation. Each Member State nominates one or two Commissioners to head the Commission. The number of nominees allocated is related to the size of the Member State.

Commissioner   One of the members of the Commission appointed by the EC Member States' governments for a four year term, which may be renewed.

Commission for Racial Equality, The   An organisation established as a result of the Race Relations Act (1976) to investigate discrimination in employment. The Commission can institute legal proceedings against persistent offenders and tries to promote equal opportunity and elimination of discrimination.

Committee   A small group of people who have been delegated powers or responsibilities.There are different forms of committees:

- **Standing** – permanent committees elected to carry out specific regular duties such as examination of finance, overseas trade policy, etc.They meet regularly and prepare reports and recommendations for management.

- **Ad hoc** – committees are elected to deal with a particular matter over a short period of time, for example, to arrange a social event.
- **Sub-committee** – a small group appointed by a committee from its members to undertake a specific task to relieve the full committee of some of its work.

Committee for Commerce and Distribution
A European Community Commission advisory body consisting primarily of representatives of retail organisations in the Member States.

Commodity Markets (Exchanges)
Markets where raw materials or foodstuffs are typically traded in bulk. Britain is a world centre for many such basic commodities.

- **Markets for commodities** – London Diamond Market, London Metal Exchange, Baltic Exchange (shipping, air transport, grain seeds and vegetable oils), London Wool Exchange, Liverpool Cotton Exchange, Liverpool Corn Exchange. In these markets the commodity is dealt with only by sample or description.
- **Wholesale produce markets (London)** – New Covent Garden (fruit and vegetables), Smithfield (meat), Billingsgate (fish). In these markets products are actually physically handled during trading.

There are specialist traders who deal on these markets:

- **Merchant** – buy on their own behalf, pay promptly and may provide their own transport.
- **Broker** – buys and sells on behalf of others on a commission (brokerage) basis.
- **'Del credere' agent** – sells on behalf of others and also guarantees payment for goods in return for extra commission.

Methods of sale on markets:

- **Private treaty** – where a commodity can be graded (for example, wheat and cotton) the seller and buyer come to a private agreement on purchase price by negotiation.
- **Auctions** – where goods vary in quality or grade (for example, tea, tobacco, wool) a representative sample is offered and buyers or their agents will bid. The purchase goes to the highest bidder.
- **Spot and 'futures'** – markets which deal in goods for immediate delivery are called 'Spot' markets because goods and payments are available immediately ('on the spot'). 'Futures' markets are those where goods are being sold for delivery and payment at some time in

the future. It is only possible to sell as a 'future' if the commodity can be graded.

Common Agricultural Policy (CAP)   A policy of the European Community which has the following objectives:

• Increased agricultural productivity
• Ensure a fair standard of living for farmers
• Stabilise markets
• Guarantee security of supplies through farm support mechanisms
• Ensure reasonable prices for consumers.

Common Commercial Policy (CCP)   The EC policy that all Member States adopt a common approach to trade with countries outside of EC memberships, for example, a common customs tariff on imports from countries outside the Community.

Common Customs Tarriff (Common External Tariff – CET)   The EC policy of all Member States imposing the same scale of charges on imports into the Community, irrespective of which Member State the goods enter.

Common Fisheries Policy (CFP)   The common arrangement for the management and conservation of fish as agreed by EC policy. It limits the 'Total Allowable Catches' of the main type of fish within quotas for each Member State. It also regulates the minimum size of fish that can be landed, and on the mesh size of nets, etc.

Common Market   (See EEC)

Communication   A means of making contact. The contact may be between people, organisations, or between places. It is the process by which businesses pass information, knowledge or items to others. Communication may take many forms; written, oral, visual, or physical movement. Methods of communication include post, telecommunication, transport and advertising.

Communication Breakdown   A situation which occurs when one or more of the four elements (transmitter, receiver, medium and message) of communication are ineffective.

Communication Network   A diagram showing the direction in which messages can be sent in an organisation.

Community Patent   An arrangement whereby a number of EC countries and some non-EC countries are signatories to the European

Patent Convention. Under this Convention, an application to patent can be made to the European Patent Office (in Munich). If the patent is granted, it is then recognised as valid by all the participating countries.

Community Trade Mark The name or mark on a product which identifies it with a particular company. Each trade mark is registered with authorities in the home country to protect them from copying or illegal use. In due course, there will be an EC-wide trade mark registration scheme.

Companies Acts 1948–85 The main laws regulating the formation, operation and winding up (closure) of companies.

Company An organisation that carries out transactions in its own name. A limited company is one in which the liability of its members is limited to the amount of share capital they have agreed to subscribe. In other words, should the company go bankrupt the shareholders are only liable to the extent of their investment and their personal property cannot be taken to make up any shortfall in the debts of the company.

- **Holding company** – a company whose main assets are shares in other companies.
- **Joint Stock Company** – another name for a limited company (see below).
- **Public Limited Company** – this type of company must include the letters PLC in its title name. It is allowed two to an unlimited number of members (owners) and it must have the minimum amount of share capital laid down in The Companies Act. The public company can advertise shares and debentures for public sale and, therefore, can raise almost limitless funds.
- **Private Limited Company** – any company not registered as a public company is a private limited company. Such a company must include Ltd or Limited in its title name. Similar to the public company this type of business is allowed two to an unlimited number of members/ shareholders. Unlike the public company the private company is not allowed to advertise shares for public sale and buyers must be found privately hence the term 'private'.

Company Prospectus A document issued by a company which invites investors to subscribe to its shares. It contains relevant financial information and the past history and future prospects of the company.

Company Secretary The person responsible for legal matters concerning a firm, and in a large firm will supervise the Legal Department.

The department's activities will include legal matters such as contracts, guarantees, insurance, compensation, etc.

Comparative Advantange   The term used when referring to one producer (or country) who is better at producing a product than another. In international trade it may be that one country is advantaged in producing a particular good due to climatic conditions.

Compensation Fee Parcels (CF)   A postal service in the UK where the Post Office will pay compensation for any parcel lost or damaged in the post if compensation fee has been paid on posting. The amount of compensation is related to the fee paid and a maximum amount. The service is not suitable for high value items which should be sent using the Registered Post service.

Compensation Fund   A fund maintained by The Stock Exchange to recompense investors should a Member Firm fail to meet its obligations. Some other organisations form similar funds. For example, the Association of British Travel Agents (ABTA) operate such a fund.

Compositional Standard   A compositional standard which specifies maximum and minimum weights of a given foodstuff, processing and cooking methods, optional ingredients, additives and minimum requirements for 'core' ingredients such as beef in beef sausages.

Comprehensive Insurance   A motor insurance which provides compensation for damage caused by the insured to the property of others and also provides compensation for accidental damage to the vehicle of the insured and property inside.

Computer   An electronic information processing machine. It can accept information from a user (input), supply information to a user (output), sort, select, store and retrieve information, and do calculations (process). The information may be in words, pictures, or numbers. Computers operate on instructions (called a program) given to them by the user. See the illustration on the opposite page.

Concentration, Geographical   A form of geographical specialisation where an industry is located in a particular area; also known as localisation.

Conciliation   Where a third party is appointed to try to help find a solution acceptable to both sides in an industrial dispute. The Advisory Conciliation and Arbitration Service (ACAS) is frequently used to bring the two sides of an industrial dispute nearer together.

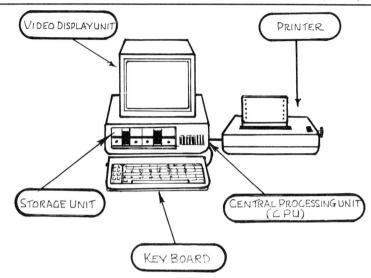

Illustration showing the various parts of the computer

Conditions of Employment   The factors which affect work such pay, hours, holidays, fringe benefits, etc. They are also known as terms of employment.

Conditions of Sale   The arrangements by which a sale is agreed, for example, quantity, price, quality, delivery, terms for payment.

Confederation of British Industry (CBI)   The major employers' organisation in the UK and it is the opposite number to the TUC (the central body of the trade union movement) The CBI represents employers and promotes the efficiency of British industry. It also provides information for its members on EC policies and proposals.

Conference Lines   Shipping lines which are bound by an agreement conference to schedule their ships on agreed routes and timetables, and to charge pre-agreed rates.

Conformity Mark   The symbol on a product which indicates that it conforms to requirements laid down by law. For example, the 'e' mark shows that a product conforms to EC legislation on weights and measures for that product.

Confravision (Video Conferencing) A conference facility provided by British Telecom which allows people to hold face-to-face discussions, but without the need for everyone to travel to the same meeting place. Studios are provided throughout the UK, which link up by sound and vision so that discussions can take place as if all those attending were present in the same room.

Modes of Presentation

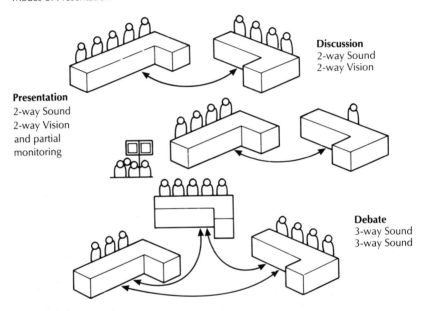

Discussion
2-way Sound
2-way Vision

Presentation
2-way Sound
2-way Vision
and partial
monitoring

Debate
3-way Sound
3-way Sound

Confravision facilities provide a variety of methods of presentation. In the near future a low-cost portable studio will allow Video Conferences to operate in a normal office or meeting room.

Conglomerate A large corporation consisting of a group of companies dealing in widely diversified goods, services, etc.

Consequential Loss Insurance A form of cover that is intended to provide financial compensation to the policy holder for any loss of business caused by an event insured against. This is sometimes referred to as business interruption insurance. For example, as a result of a fire business may have to be suspended causing a loss additional to that resulting from the fire damage, and perhaps requiring wages to still be paid. Insurance cover is available for such losses.

Consideration The money value of a Stock Exchange transaction.

Consignee The person to whom goods are being sent.

Consignment A quantity of goods being sent to a consignee.

Consignment Note A document provided by the transporter of goods. The consignor fills in the form with details of the consignment, for example, number of packages, details of consignee, etc. The consignment note accompanies the goods during transit and the consignee signs it to acknowledge receipt.

Consignor The person sending goods to a consignee.

Consols The stocks issued by the UK government with fixed rate of interest but no stated date of maturity.

Consular Invoice An invoice which has been signed by the Consul or the country to which they have been sent to certify that it shows the correct price. This is necessary when an import tax is being applied based on the value of the goods in question.

Consular Officials Public officials appointed by governments to reside in foreign countries to look after the interests of compatriates. They also collect information that is of interest to businessmen intending to trade overseas.

Consultative Councils Councils which have been set up in the UK to protect the interests of consumers who use state owned industries. They are set up by Parliament but they are independent of the industry. They deal with complaints by consumers and they represent consumers in the formation of policies, for example, Post Office Users' National Council.

Consumer A person who buys and uses goods or services to satisfy his own wants. The consumer is the final link in the chain of distribution.

Consumer Advice Centres Locally situated centres which provide shoppers with information and advice related to the purchase of goods or services. They are set up by local authorities to deal with consumer problems and Citizen Advice Bureaux will often refer consumers to them for advice and help on specific problems.

Consumer Credit Act 1974 An Act of the UK Parliament to control all forms of credit services. It includes regulation of credit and hire agreements, licensing of lenders, advertisements offering credit facilities, breaches of agreements, extortionate charges and credit referencing. The Act protects the consumer in the following ways:

- All businesses involved with credit or hire agreements are required to obtain a licence from the Office of Fair Trading.
- Consumers can ask a court to reduce unfair or extortionate rates of interest.
- Individuals can ask to see the contents of files referring to them held by credit reference agencies which supply information about the financial standing of people. The individual can ask for incorrect information to be corrected.
- All relevant information must be brought to the notice of the borrower. Advertisements offering credit should not be misleading and must advise the consumer of the annual percentage rate (APR), i.e. the true rate of interest.
- Compensation may be claimed for goods that are faulty.

Consumer Durables Goods such as televisions, cookers, etc. which are used by consumers many times and are expected to last for a long period of time.

Consumer Goods Products bought by households to satisfy their needs. They will either be used up within a year (single use), or will last for more than a year (consumer durable).

Consumer Legislation Laws which protect the interests of the consumer when buying goods or services for cash or on credit.

Consumer Protection The variety of means that exist to protect the consumer against poor quality of goods or services and unscrupulous salespeople. Consumer protection ultimately lies in various laws that exist, but it is supported by various independent organisations, government and local authority bodies, industry and trade organisations.

Consumer Safety Act 1978 An Act of the UK Parliament which regulates the sale of goods that are potentially dangerous, for example, electrical goods, cooking equipment, heaters, toys etc.

Consumer Sovereignty A situation where consumers tell producers what to produce, rather than producers dictating to consumers what they can and cannot buy.

Consumers' Association A non-profit making organisation which is financed by members' subscriptions. it carries out comparative tests on goods and services, the results of which are published in the association's magazine called *Which?*. The association also publishes well researched books on consumer-related matters.

Consumers' Co-operative A co-operative set up by a group of consumers to obtain benefits of bulk buying. The owners and employees are also its regular customers.

Containerisation A method of transporting goods in a large metal box as opposed to using individual cartons. The containers come in two International Standards Organisation (ISO) sizes of 20 or 40 foot length. The container is packed at the factory or at an inland pooling depot. The container can be loaded quickly and precisely into position on a lorry, train, ship or aircraft by a single process using special lifting equipment. Handling costs are reduced and so are risks of damage or loss of goods.

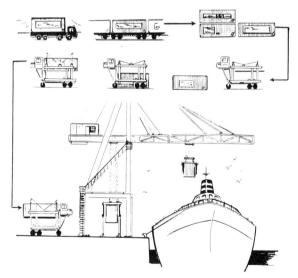

Containers will enter the port by road or rail. They are moved around the port by 'straddle' carriers and loaded precisely in and out of the vessel by special cranes, keeping labour involvement to a minimum.

Contango A Stock Exchange term which refers to the arrangement whereby a 'bull' or a 'bear' can carry over their position in a security from one account to another without paying for or delivering the stock. The term 'contango' is also used to refer to the charge paid for this delay in payment.

Contract A legally binding agreement between two or more people that they will or will not do something.

Contract Note A Stock Exchange term for the document which summarises a transaction that a Broker has carried out on behalf of a client. It shows the following:

- The date the buying or selling was carried out
- The identity and number of shares involved
- The amount the client must pay or will receive
- How much commission the Broker is charging

A BROKER & CO. A. K. WOOD T. S. JONES J. R. SMITH	99 Throgmorton Street LONDON EC2X 1AC *Telephone:* 01 432 8114 *Telex:* 44259

MISS ANN BUYER
94 THE CRESCENT
HORSHAM
WEST SUSSEX RH12 1NB

V.A.T. Registration No.
3437 123 64 9428

Bargain Date	Security	Client	Account	Contract Ref.	Settlement
31 OCT 2005			22 (v)		18 NOV 2005

We thank you for your instructions and have this day BOUGHT

BAILEY MARINE PLC   ORDINARY 50p SHARES

Quantity	Price	Consideration
2000	58p	1160·00

TRANSFER STAMP	(n)	6.00
COMMISSION (1.65%)		19.14
VAT (15%)		2.87

A Broker + Co

TOTAL
£1188.01

Subject to the Rules, Regulations and Usages of the Stock Exchange   MEMBERS OF THE STOCK EXCHANGE

V.A.T. Invoice for services rendered. (N) = Not subject to V.A.T.   CAPITAL GAINS TAX. We recommend that Contract Notes be retained for future reference.
E. & O. E.   (D) = Commission divisible with yourselves

Contract of Employment   A law which requires employers to give employees particulars of their terms of employment within 13 weeks of starting work. The contract will include details of pay, conditions, holidays, etc.

Contribution   An amount of money which insurers are liable to meet a claim against a policy. They each contribute an amount towards the loss in proportion to the fraction of the risk they agreed to cover.

Convenience Foods   Pre-packed foodstuffs which require a minimum of preparation before they are eaten.

Convertible Bank Note   A bank note which can be exchanged for gold.

Convertible Preference Share   A share which can be converted into an ordinary share at a certain time or upon paying a certain sum.

Conveyancing   The complicated procedure of correctly transferring property ownership from one person to another. When buying or selling property, people usually pay a solicitor to do the conveyancing.

Co-operatives   A term used when small units of business within production, agriculture or retailing, owned by people with limited amounts of capital, combine together for the purpose of sharing labour and buying or hiring equipment which individually they would be unable to afford. By co-operating in this way the members of the co-operative not only have access to the economic use of equipment, but they also enjoy economies of scale such as bulk purchasing, joint advertising or marketing.

COPOLCO   Consumer Policy Committee of the International Organisation for Standardisation (ISO). COPOLCO helps to make international standards as relevant as possible to consumer needs.

Copyright   The exclusive right to produce copies and to control an original literary, musical, or artistic work.

Corporation Tax   The tax paid by limited companies, owned by sharcholders on the amount of profit declared in any one year. Similar to individuals and income tax, companies are allowed to deduct certain expenditure as tax-free allowances from their gross profit and the remaining net profit is liable for tax.

Correction Signs   The standard signs used to indicate that changes need to be made to text. It is sometimes necessary in business to read text or drafts of typewritten material and note amendments or corrections which are required to be made. The main methods are shown here.

Correction	Sign in margin	Sign in text
Insert full stop	⊙/	⎜
Insert comma	7	⎜
Insert question mark	?/	⎜
Insert apostrophe	⋅7	⎜
Use capital letters	Caps/	≡
Insert word(s)	words/	⎜
Use italics	ital/	————
Use lower case letters	l c /	encircle (letter(s))
Transpose (to change the order of) words or letters	trs/	⎍ ⎚
Delete (get rid of)	⌐7	letters crossed out
To remain as it was	stet/	dotted line under words wrongly struck through
Space required	#/	⎜
Close up the space	⌒/	⌒
Start a new paragraph	N.P./	⎾

We are writing to te̶l̶l̶ you ab̶o̶u̶t a special
promotion a̶t offer we are giving to existing
customers over the next 4̶ ̶w̶e̶e̶k̶s̶.[As from
the begining of of next month we are adding
footwear to our range of products.⌐
    ⎾An illustrated brochure/is included with
this letter, and we are sure that you will find
the prices q̶u̶o̶t̶e̶d̶ very competitive/for
one just month from the introduction of the
new Range we are offering existing
customers a 10% discount/additional to our
standing 25% trade discount.

Margin annotations: advise/ ⊙7 month/ n/ ⌒ stet trs/ l.c.

Right margin annotations: of/ # N.P. ∧ and price list ⊙/ N.P./ cap/ ⌒/ (7)/ ital/

Cost and Freight (C & F)   The price quoted for supply includes cost of goods and transport charges.

Cost-benefit Analysis   The process of looking at the private costs and benefits and the social costs and benefits of a particular project. The private costs and benefits are financial ones faced by the businesses involved. The social costs and benefits are faced by the community as a whole, and may not be readily measured in financial terms, for example, the inconvenience to a section of a community of having a motorway built near homes.

Cost, Insurance and Freight (CIF)   Price of goods is the same as C & F but also includes freight insurance costs.

Cost of Living Index   (See Index of Retail Prices Costs)

Costs   What a business spends in order to provide goods or services for its customers.

Council of Ministers   The Council of the European Community (EC) which consists of one Minister from each EC Member State and is the final decision-taking body of the EC. Although reference is normally made to 'the Council' there are in fact different Councils for different areas of policy.

Counterfoil   The stub of a cheque or bank paying-in slip.

Cover Note   A document providing temporary evidence of insurance cover while the policy is being prepared.

Credit   Credit refers to a situation where one person allows another some financial benefit over a period of time. For example, selling on credit means allowing a buyer the use of goods whilst paying for them over a period of time by regular instalments.

- **Bank Credit** – banks allow suitable customers credit in a variety of ways, for example, loans, overdrafts, etc. These are examined at the appropriate points elsewhere in this dictionary.
- **Trade Credit** – occurs where a trader allows another to have goods and pay for them after an agreed period of time for example, at the end of the month. This allows the buyer the opportunity of selling the goods before they have paid for them.
- **Hire Purchase (HP) Agreement** – goods are 'hired' by the purchaser until full repayment has been completed, often including payment of interest but sometimes interest-free. The goods do not become the

property of the buyer until final payment has been made and if the buyer defaults on repayment the finance company can repossess the goods within certain restrictions imposed by the Consumer Credit Act.

- **Credit Sale Agreement** – this is similar to a HP agreement but goods become the property of the buyer immediately the deposit or the first payment is made. If the buyer defaults on the regular repayments the finance company cannot repossess the goods but can sue the buyer for the outstanding amount in a Court of Law.

- **Charge Cards** – some retailers operate their own form of credit whereby they issue customers charge cards which allow purchases within the company's shops and charge the items to their personal account. The system is frequently linked to an instalment system operated by the firm, sometimes interest-free.

- **Credit Cards** – the holder of a credit card can make purchases up to a set amount without paying by cash or cheque. The trader claims the money for the purchase from the company that has issued the credit card. The card holder is in due course presented with a demand for payment, which can usually be made over a period of time (for example, American Express, Access).

[1]If goods are supplied subject to defects these should be listed.	SCHEDULE Particulars of the goods sufficient to identify them[1]	Cash Price	
		£	p

	Terms of payment:
	    payments of **£**
	per payable on the day
	(in monthly payments not the
	29th, 30th or 31st)
	of each commencing 19
	[and one payment of **£**
	One thereafter] (delete if not required)
		Total Cash Price of Goods
		Less Part Exchange **£** :
		    Cash Deposit **£** :
		= Total amount payable on
		Buyer signing		

		Balance of Cash Price		
		Add Hire purchase Charge		
		Balance of Hire Purchase Price		
		Hire Purchase Price		

Credit Control

A method that a business will use to decide whether it will grant credit facilities. There are a variety of forms of credit control. A firm wishing to obtain credit from a supplier may offer the name of a well-known firm with whom they have had previous dealings as a reference (trade reference). Another method of credit control is for the seller to consult a credit reference agency who keep records of firms and individuals who default on payments.

Credit Insurance   A system operated by insurance companies to help exporters.

Credit Note   A document sent by the seller to the buyer to correct an overcharge or to give a refund. It has the effect of reducing a charge made. There many reasons why a trader might issue a credit note:

- An invoicing error has resulted in the customer being overcharged.
- Some of the goods have been returned as faulty.
- Too few goods were delivered.
- Refund on returned packing.

CREDIT NOTE			**CN 566**

CANDIDA PLC
CLOTHING MANUFACTURING
49 Sanquar Road, London E17 3XB
Tel: 081-315-1234 Fax 081-315-1243

Date 12th February 199-

Smart Wear Limited
147 Cheatle Road
London SE16 1SD

Credit against
Order No. 01797   **Dated** 3rd February
Invoice no. 10862   **Dated** 9th February

Quantity		Price	Amount
10	by allowance against packing cases returned	2.42	£24.20

E & OE

Creditor   People to whom a business owes money.

Credit Reference Agency   (See Credit Control)

Credit Sale Agreement   (See Credit)

Credit Slip/Paying in Slip
A form filled in when paying money into a bank account. The counterfoil is endorsed by the cashier and retained by account holder as proof of inpayment.

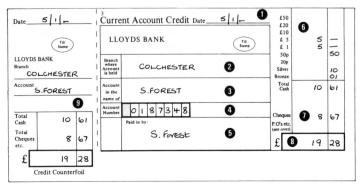

1 Date, 2 Name of account holding branch, 3 Account holder's name, 4 Account Number, 5 Signature of person paying money in, 6 Breakdown of cash paid in, 7 Amount of cheques paid in, 8 Total of the credit to the account (cash or cheques), 9 Counterfoil

This credit slip will have both parts stamped and signed by the bank cashier. The bank will take the larger section to use in updating the customer's account.

Credit Squeeze
A term referring to a Government policy of restricting availability of credit. As a result of such a policy borrowing becomes more expensive and more difficult to obtain.

Credit Transfer
(See Bank Giro)

Cumulative Preference Share
Shareholders who have a priority claim on the profits of a company after debenture holders. Ordinary preference shares pay a fixed rate of dividend but only if sufficient profits are available to make the payment. Cumulative preference shareholders who do not receive their full dividend in one year have the amount due to them accumulated until sufficient profits are available to pay them.

Currency
Another term for money e.g. banknotes, coins, cheques and bills of exchange. Currency is any accepted method of payment.

Current Account (Bank)
A type of bank account on which the customer can draw cheques. It is referred to as a current account because money in the account is immediately available.

Current Assets (See Assets)

Curriculum Vitae (CV) A brief recent history of an applicant for a job. It should include education, qualifications, relevant experience, etc. This may be typed or written to accompany a letter of application, thus making it possible to make the letter shorter and more concise.

Curriculum Vitae

Name	Alison Louise Killick
Address	24 Farmer Street, Bournemouth, BH2 6PX
Nationality	British
Marital status	Single
Date of birth	24th December 1976
Education	Blue Ridge Comprehensive School, Bournemouth (1978–1993)
Qualifications	(Awaiting examination results)
GCSE:	English, Mathematics, Science, Technology, Geography, French, Business Studies
Experience	One week of work experience at Hart Insurance Company, Bournemouth, dealing with incoming and outgoing mail and filing. Business Studies course at school involved operating the school reception desk. Saturday part-time work at Godfrey's Hardware Store, Bournemouth, dealing with customers and maintaining stock records.
Hobbies	Gardening, reading, music
Other interests	Helping in the day centre for old people
References	These may be obtained from: The Headmaster, Blue Ridge Comprehensive School, Bournemouth The Manager, Godfrey's Hardware Store, Bournemouth

---

Cursor A small illuminated area shown on a computer screen. It shows where the next typed character will appear. The cursor can be moved to any position in a document in order to type in corrections or type new text.

Customs The collection of import taxes.

Customs Declaration Form A form which must be completed when sending goods out of or receiving goods into the country. The form is issued by the government for statistical purposes.

Customs Duties   (See Duties)

Customs Union   An agreement between countries to remove or reduce trade barriers between them in order to promote trade. The European Community is working towards a customs union.

CWO   An abbreviation which stands for 'cash with order' and is used to indicate that a seller requires payment before supply of goods or services.

Daily Settlement   The daily settlement of indebtedness between the clearing banks.

Daisy Wheel   A computer printer which prints via a 'wheel' with typeface segments. It produces letter-quality printout similar to type-script. It generally it prints at a slower speed than a dot matrix printer.

Data   A collection of facts, figures or information in the form of digits, characters or symbols available for human analysis or by computer.

Data Bank   A collection of facts, figures or information which can be retrieved for research and analysis, usually by computer.

Database   A specific collection of information in a series of files stored in a computer in a manner whereby they can be accessed in a variety of ways. It has some similarity with a filing cabinet with file folders, and each file folder containing information. The database file contains records, with each record containing data fields. Just as the file folders in a filing cabinet are related to each other in some way, so are the records in a database file. Each contains similar information. A business might use a database to record its daily sales by departments over a given period. The information collected in this way could then be summarised in a table, graph or chart and used in comparison with previous or predicted sales.

Data Management   A computing term used to refer to systems that manipulate data automatically and present it in a form that enables logical analysis to be carried out.

Datapost   A postal service in the UK providing a fast, secure, highly reliable courier delivery service for urgent packages. Datapost travels separately from ordinary mail and is handled by special staff. There are various categories of the service, for example, Datapost sameday, Datapost overnight.

Data Preparation   The series of processes that information goes through before it is in a form that a computer can understand.

Data Processing   The process of recording and analysing large amounts of information by computer into pre-planned formats.

Dated Stock   Government securities carrying a maturation date.

Datel   A telecommunications system which allows a computer in a firm to communicate with computers in other parts of the country, and in many overseas countries.

Day Book   Accounts recording details of daily transactions, such as sales.

Day Release   A system of in-service training whereby employees are allowed a day each week away from work, usually on full pay, to attend a college or some other educational establishment.

Dealer   A person dealing on their own account and not acting as an agent for another person.

Death Rate   The number of deaths per thousand of population per year. It can also be expressed as a percentage figure.

Debenture   A certificate issued by a company stating the amount owed by the company to the bearer of the certificate. It carries a fixed interest, which is payable either yearly or half-yearly and a maturity date, which is when the capital borrowed by the company is to be returned. Debentures can be bought and sold in the stock market. A debenture holder is a creditor, not an owner of the company.

Debit   An accounting entry that increases a charge against a person or an account.

Debit Note   A document sent to correct an amount due if the amount stated in a previous invoice was too low.

Debt   Money, goods or services owed to others.

Debt, Bad   A debt that has little or no prospect of being repaid.

Debt Capital (Loan Capital)   Money loaned to a business on a long-term (at least one year) basis. Providers of debt capital are creditors of the firm and normally receive interest in the return for the loan.

Debt Collection   The process of recovering money owed by debtors. Some firms specialise in this type of work, acting as agents for others.

Debt Counselling   Giving advice to debtors about repayment of debts where they are experiencing difficulty, for example, suggesting order of priority or methods of negotiating deferred payments.

Debt Factoring   An arrangement which aims to increase the rate of flow of cash into an organisation. Under the arrangement a factoring house 'buys' a firm's (the client's) trade debts as they occur. When the client issues the invoice the factor pays up to 80 per cent of the debt after deducting charges. The balance of 20 per cent is paid by the factor to the client when the customer pays the factor. This saves the firm from having to wait to get its money.

Debt Finance   The raising of money by borrowing from people who are not owners of the business.

Debtor   A person who owes another person money. In the case of a business this is usually customers who have purchased on credit.

Debt Ratio   A comparative tool used in the analysis of financial statements to show the relationship of debts to assets – the amount of protection available for creditors. Debt ratio is calculated by dividing the amount of total debt by the amount of the net worth of the business.

Debt Servicing   The payment of interest on a debt.

Debugging   The identification and removal of errors from a computer program or the elimination of faults from the system.

Decentralisation   The method by which large organisations delegate authority to several sub-units such as departments. Centralisation of business organisation and operations can lead to poor communication and ineffective control.

Declared Dividend   A return that is formally authorised by a firm's board of directors for payment on a specified date to holders of a security registered on that date.

Declaration of Solvency   A formal sworn statement by the directors of a company verifying that when the firm closes down all debts will be repaid in a given time not exceeding one year.

Decreasing Term Policy   A life insurance policy for a specified period in which the amount payable on the death of the assured decreases as the term progresses.

Deed A formal legal document signed, sealed, and delivered to effect a conveyance or transfer of property or to create a legal obligation or contract.

Deed of Covenant An agreement whereby a contributor agrees to pay a fixed sum for a period of seven years, usually to a charitable organisation. If the beneficiary is approved by the Inland Revenue tax benefits can be gained.

Deed of Partnership A deed which outlines the rights and relationships between the members of a partnership.

Defalcation The embezzlement of money.

Default The failure to pay debt, interest or principal when due.

Default Notice A notice which specifies the nature of a breach of a credit agreement and how it can be remedied.

Defective Title Where a person believes he has ownership of a title but there is some imperfection in his claim to ownership.

Deferred Payments (See Credit Sales Agreement)

Deferred Stocks or Shares Stocks or shares which do not entitle the holders to any dividend until a fixed rate has been paid to holders of preference and ordinary shares.

Defendant A person against whom an action or claim is brought in a court of law.

Deficiency Where liabilities exceed assets, or where expenditure exceeds income.

Deficit Where there is a loss, for example, balance of trade or balance of payments – a minus currency outflow.

Deflation A persistent reduction in general level of prices throughout the country. It can indicate a stagnation or reduction in economic activity.

Del Credere Agent A type of broker involved in foreign trade who guarantees the owner that the goods, for which he is the agent, will be sold. In giving this guarantee the broker undertakes a risk and, therefore, his commission is higher than an ordinary broker's.

Delegation The passing down to subordinates the authority to take decisions, but keeping overall responsibility for those decisions.

Delivery Costs   A statement of the extent to which charges for delivery have been included in price. This can be quoted in a number of ways:

- **Cost and freight (c & f)** – This covers the cost of goods, and freight, with the buyer having to make his own insurance arrangements.
- **Cost, insurance and freight (c, i & f)** – The same as above but including the cost of transit insurance.
- **Ex works** – The price covers the goods at the factory, all additional costs (transport, etc) being the responsibility of the buyer.
- **Franco** – The price includes all costs up to and included delivery to the premises of the customer (usually overseas).
- **Free on board (fob)** – Price includes delivery to and onboard a ship.
- **Free on rail (for)** – Price includes delivery to and onto a railway vehicle.

(See also Delivery, Terms of)

Delivery Note   A note accompanying goods being delivered. The original is given to the receiver who checks that the goods listed in the note have been received; a copy is signed by the receiver to acknowledge his receipt of the goods.

Delivered Price   A quoted or invoice price that includes delivery costs.

Delivery Orders   The orders given by the owners of goods left at a warehouse instructing the warehouse keeper to deliver the goods to a certain destination.

Delivery Period   A statement included in a quotation from a supplier to a buyer indicating when delivery will take place.

Delivery, Terms of   Quotations from seller to buyer indicate whether buyer or seller is to pay for the cost of packing and delivery of goods:

- **Carriage forward** – the cost of transport to be paid by consignee.
- **Carriage paid** – the cost of transport is paid by consignor.

Demand   1) A request for payment of outstanding debt. 'Final demand' refers to a final request for payment which unless responded to will result in legal action.   2) The amount of a product or service that consumers are willing and able to buy over a time period. Demand is influenced by many factors such as the tastes and preferences of consumers, their income, which in turn may be affected by a change in the distribution of incomes within the economy. Population changes also influence demand. An increase in the birthrate will have a continuing effect on demand for goods and services until the bulge eventually disappears upon the death of the particular age group involved. Demand is also affected by the competition and substitute products available.

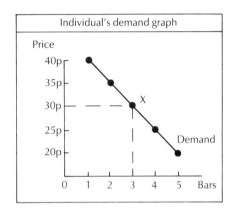

Individual's demand schedule	
Price of each chocolate bar	Quantity demanded at each price
40p	1
35p	2
30p	3
25p	4
20p	5

An individual's demand schedule and demand graph for chocolate bars at various prices. The point x on this demand curve indicates that at a price of 30p the person would be likely to buy three bars.

Demand Deposit   A deposit in a commercial bank that can be withdrawn without notice to the bank; it is payable on demand to the depositor.

Demand and Supply, Laws of   An increase or decrease in demand or supply leading to a rise or fall in price. Under perfect competition, price is decided by the interaction of demand and supply; the market price is the price that where demand and supply are in equilibrium, i.e. the goods supplied by producers equals the quantity bought by consumers. (See also Supply) See the illustration on page 62.

Demand Draft   A draft drawn by a branch bank on the bank's head office. Being drawn on itself, it is accepted as the equivalent of cash.

Demarcation Dispute   A dispute is one where 'who does what' is in question, and is often a dispute between groups of members of different unions. It is a situation where one group of workers object to another group doing particular work.

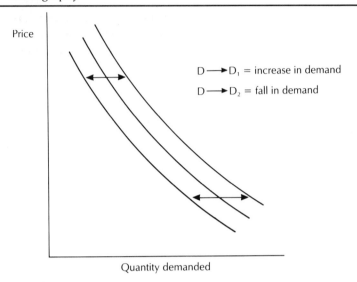

A change in the quantity demanded causes a shift in the demand curve.

Demography   The science of population statistics. It is the social study of people in their communities. It draws on data relating to births, deaths, marriage etc., to draw conclusions about human behaviour.

Demurrage   A charge made by the carrier of goods (for example, the ship owner) if the goods are not unloaded within a stated time.

Department   A specialised division of a large organisation such as a business.

Department of Employment   A department of the UK government responsible for manpower planning, youth and adult vocational training, and policy on racial and sexual equality in employment.

Department of Trade and Industry   A department of the UK government with responsibility for policy decisions related to company and commercial law, foreign trade, and regional development.

Department Store   A large retail store selling a wide range of goods, divided into separate trading departments, each of which specialises in a class of goods and is expected to show individual profitability.

Dependent   A person who is supported by a taxpayer.

Dependency Ratio   The dependency ratio is the proportion of the working population to the non-working (dependent) population;

$$\frac{\text{Number of workers}}{\text{Number of dependents}} = \text{Dependency Ratio}$$

Depleted Cost   The cost that remains after deductions for accrued depletion have been made. This term is normally applied to items such as minerals, coal, oil and natural gas, etc.

Depletion   The reduction or exhaustion of a natural resource. This concept is normally applied to mineral deposits, standing timber, natural gas, coal, oil, etc.

Deposit   Cheques, coin, currency, bonds, drafts and other items that are deposited with a bank for credit to an account.

Deposit Account   An account for savings which earns interest and is generally meant for safekeeping of funds not required for immediate use.

Depositors   People who deposit money in a bank or deposit-taking company.

Deposit-taking Institutions   Smaller institutions which are recognised as deposit-taking institutions. The term 'bank' is restricted to institutions offering a full banking service and who have been registered as banks.

Depreciation   The fall in value or usefulness of an item due to use and ageing. It is a term used in relation the process of reducing the value of the assets of a firm. The purpose of depreciation is to reduce the cost of fixed assets to a scrap or realistic value because they cannot be restored by repair because of wear, obsolescence or inadequacy.

Depressed Areas   An area or region characterised by relative economic hardship and high unemployment.

Depression   A term sometimes used to describe a time of low economic activity and protracted unemployment.

Deregulation   The process of removing legislative requirements and restrictions on industry which may be regarded as restricting economic activity or limiting competition.

Design Centre   An exhibition of goods in the UK which have been selected by the Council of Industrial Design for their good design and quality. The centre is sited in London.

Desk Research   An advertising tool which involves an analysis of statistics that are already available to the organisation. This data could include details of past sales and other information useful for assisting marketing strategies, but can also draw on data outside of the organisation such as those included in wide public surveys, for example, 'Social Trends'.

Destination Principle   A policy agreed by the EC which rules that Value Added Tax should be collected in the country where goods are finally sold rather than in the country where they originate.

Devaluation   A reduction in the value of a currency in relation to the value of other currencies. Devaluation can have the effect of restricting imports because they in effect become more expensive to buy. Devaluation may be brought about by deliberate government action.

Development Area or Region   Areas of high unemployment and declining basic industries that the Government have identified as needing support such as grants and subsidies.

Dictating Machine   A machine used to make an audio recording of material to be typed, for example, messages, letters, reports, speeches, etc.

Differential (Wage)   A term which refers to the difference between the amount one group earns when compared with another.

Diminishing Returns   An economic reference to a situation where progressively smaller increases in output result from equal increases in production.

Diplomas Directive   A European Community ruling that people with professional qualifications gained after three or more years of study can practice anywhere within the Community without having to requalify locally.

Direct Cost   A term used in cost accounting to refer to all expenditure which can be attributed to production, or a segment of business operations such as labour, material, and overheads. These costs vary with the volume of production.

Direct Dealing   (See Direct Selling)

Direct Debit   An authorisation given by the account holder of a bank to a third party to withdraw money from that account at any time up to a specific date limit.

Direct Labour Cost   That portion of labour that is applied directly to a product.

Direct Liability   The obligation of a debtor to another person.

Direct Mail   Material such as advertising leaflets sent direct to the potential customer through the post.

Director   A person chosen by shareholders to represent them in the running of a company. They form a 'board of directors' who decide major company policy.

Direct Production   The changing of raw materials into goods in one single process without any help from others (i.e. without specialisation).

Direct Sales   The selling by producer straight to the customer without using any intermediary such as a retailer.

Direct Service   An occupation which is not involved in production or commerce but is provided directly to the consumer, for example, teachers, doctors, police, entertainers.

Direct Tax   A tax paid by the person or organisation on which it is levied, for example, Income Tax, and Corporation Tax. By comparison indirect taxes are those charged on goods and services, for example, Value Added Tax.

Dirty Money   An additional payment made to workers for handling objectionable items.

Discharge   To carry out a duty or obligation, or to terminate an obligation. It is a term that is also used to refer to the termination of employment by an employer.

Discharged Bankrupt   A person who has been declared a bankrupt and is now released from the restrictions imposed by bankruptcy having convinced a Court that all reasonable efforts have been made to settle outstanding debts.

Disclaimer   A repudiation or denial of any connection, duty or obligation.

Disclose   To make information known openly.

Discount   To deduct a specified amount from the usual price of a product or service.

- **Cash discount** – offered to customers to encourage prompt payment of outstanding debt.
- **Quantity discount** – related to the quantity purchased; the rate of discount will depend upon quantity purchased.
- **Trade discount** – allowed to people in the same trade as the seller to enable them to make a profit on resale of the goods.

Discount House   An institution specialising in making short-term loans by buying bills at a discount on their value, using money borrowed from other institutions.

Discounting   1) The process of buying something at a price lower than its nominal value, with the purpose of selling it later at a profit.   2) The purchase of a credit instrument, for example, bill of exchange or promissory note, for a sum less than the face value.

Discount Market   The part of the finance market that is concerned with short-term borrowing.

Discount Store   A shop which specialises in selling at cut prices.

Discretionary Cost   A cost that is not essential to the management of a business. It is also known as escapable or avoidable cost.

Discretionary Trust   A trust where the trustee has the right to use his own judgement in respect of investments so long as they are reasonable and without undue risk.

Diseconomies of Scale   The problems of management organisation and communication which arise when a business grows in size. It results in a rise in unit costs.

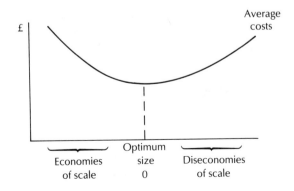

Operating on a large scale has many advantages in that increase in size or output generally results in a fall in unit costs (economies of scale). But large scale operations do not necessarily always result in reduced costs. For example, increased growth may also result in inefficiencies creeping into the organisation, causing unit costs to rise (diseconomies of scale). The ideal situation is where a firm uses resources in the best way and produces as economically as possible. Where this occurs it is the optimum size of the firm.

Dishonour   To refuse acceptance or payment by the drawee of cheques or other commercial papers.

Dishonoured Cheque   A cheque on which a bank has refused payment. It may be that there are insufficient funds in the account, but it can also be for a number of other reasons such as, the cheque has not been signed, the signature differs from the example held by the bank, or the drawer may themselves have stopped the payment.

Dishonour of a Bill   A bill of exchange may be dishonoured because the drawee refuses to accept the bill, or an acceptor fails to pay when it is due.

Disk (Computer)   A storage medium used to hold computer data. It is a flat circular disk coated with magnetic material. It can be flexible or hard.

Dismissal   An employer ending the contract of employment of an employee. The worker can appeal against unfair dismissal by employers.

Dispatch Note   A note sent by the seller to the buyer to tell them that goods have been sent to them.

Disposable Income   The amount of income available after taxes have been paid.

Dissolution   The termination of a meeting, or formal or legal agreement.

Distributed Profit   That part of profit shared out by a company between its shareholders and referred to as a dividend.

Distribution   The process of getting finished products from the producer to the consumer, including storage, transport, customer relations, credit arrangements, retail and wholesale trading.

Distribution Channels (Distribution Network)   The traders that form the 'chain of distribution', for example, producer, wholesaler, retailer, consumer. (See also Chain of Distribution)

Distribution Costs   Costs incurred to promote the sale and to facilitate the movement of goods into the hands of purchasers.

Distribution Mix   The pattern of distribution used by a business; different products will require different methods of distribution.

Distributive Trades   Those whose business is the distribution of goods. (See also Distribution Channels)

Diversification   The expansion of the range of goods and services into other areas or activities. Such diversification can reduce or spread the risks faced by a firm.

Dividend   The amount of profit that the directors of a business decide to distribute to their shareholders in a year. The 'rate of dividend' is the amount given for each share held.

- **Mandate** – The authorisation by a stockholder for a company to pay a dividend direct to a specified bank account.
- **Warrant** – The cheque by which a dividend is paid.

Division of Labour   The method by which people co-operate with others to indirectly produce the needs of everyone. This is often referred to as division of labour or specialisation. In modern society few people satisfy their needs directly. Work is divided among several people, allowing them each to specialise in doing what they do best, which is to the benefit of everyone. There are two main ways of looking at specialisation:

1) **Specialisation by product**
Instead of everyone trying to produce all they personally need, they each concentrate on contributing to one commodity or service, using the money that they earn to purchase the goods or services of others. In this way the total needs of an individual are met by the contributions of many others.

2) **Specialisation by process**
By organising production into several stages or processes workers become more specialised and expert in their work. For example, in a car factory each worker might specialise in a part of the assembly of many vehicles in one day as they pass along the production line. By organising production in this way, workers become more

specialised and expert in their work. This enables them to produce more with the same resources.

Docket A piece of paper accompanying or referring to a package or other delivery, stating contents, delivery instructions, etc., sometimes serving as a receipt, and sometimes as a notice of contents for Customs purposes.

Document A piece of paper, booklet, etc., providing information of an official or legal nature.

Document Retention Period The length of time that a business decides to retain documents on file. The document retention period will depend upon the amount of filing space the firm has available and the nature of the documentation. Some documents must be kept on file for a minimum period to meet legal requirements, for example, company accounts and records of accidents to employees.

Document of Title A document which provides evidence that the holder is the legal owner of goods.

Documentary Bill A bill of exchange being used as part of a collection of documents which an exporter sends through a bank with certain shipping documents.

Documentary Credit An arrangement whereby a bank in an exporter's country is authorised by the importer to make a payment or to accept a bill of exchange upon presentation of documentary evidence that the goods have been shipped.

Domestic Trade The purchase and sale of goods within a country.

Domicile The place where a person has their permanent home.

Donation A gift, usually to a charitable, religious, or educational institution, that can be deducted from gross income for taxation purposes.

Doorstep Selling Selling direct to consumers at their door. The Sales Away from Business Premises Directive of the EC protects consumers from unscrupulous or high pressure door-to-door selling by allowing a seven day 'cooling off' period during which signed agreements on purchases above a certain value made 'at the home' can be cancelled by the consumer.

Door-to-Door   Transport from one door to another; a complete collection and delivery service.

Dormant Partner   (See Sleeping Partner)

Dot-Matrix Printer   A computer line printer which produces characters made up of a series of small dots. This method of printing is faster than a daisy wheel printer, and allows the easy formation of a variety of typefaces, and graphic displays.

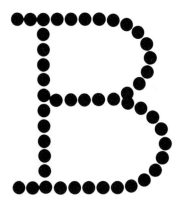

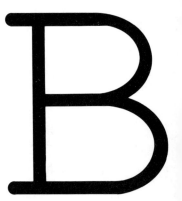

The letter B printed by a dot matrix printer

The letter B printed by a letter-quality printer

Double Coincidence of Wants   When two people wish to exchange an item (for example, by barter) and there is complete agreement between them; each wants what the other has to offer.

Dow Jones Index   An index compiled by the Dow Jones Company in the USA showing movements in the price of 30 leading industrial shares in the USA. It is the US equivalent of the UK Financial Times Index.

Draft   A written order, such as a cheque, drawn by one party ordering a second party (for example, a bank) to pay to a third party. The term can also be used to refer to a preliminary outline of a proposed document.

Drawback   A repayment of customs or excise duty when goods that have been taxed upon entry to the country are re-exported.

Drawee 1) The person to whom a document is addressed, for example, in a bill of exchange, the drawee is the one who has to pay the money, in the case of a cheque it is the bank against whom the cheque is drawn. 2) The person who writes up or drafts a document, for example, in a bill of exchange.

Drawer The account holder who signs a cheque.

Drip Advertising A continuous programme of advertising over an extended period, for example, twelve months.

Dry Run A rehearsal or trial of part of an advertising campaign.

Duplicating The making of exact copies of originals using a master copy such as a stencil or an art master.

Dumping The selling goods at a loss abroad. Some countries will 'dump' abroad either to reduce supplies at home (to maintain price levels) or to increase their share of the market overseas. This can be harmful to industries in the country where the goods are being dumped.

Duties Taxes imposed on foreign goods entering a country. They are levied to protect home trade, to raise revenue for the Government, and sometimes to reduce consumption for ethical or economic reasons. They are collected by Customs and Excise officials.

E The symbol E (for Europe) is used in a variety of forms to indicate that a product conforms to EC legislative requirements. The following are examples:

- e – shows that a product conforms to the agreed EC system for average weights and measures.
- ε – the Greek letter e or epsilon, printed backwards, indicates that an aerosol conforms to the requirements of the EC.
- E10 – in this particular case the E and number indicates a package is one of the standard capacity sizes for boxes of washing powder.

E & O E (See Errors and Ommissions Excepted)

E Number A number which is given to a food additive, e.g E211, preservatives, and E102, tartrazine. The E stands for EC and indicates that the additive is one of those regulated by the Community.

E111 A form which entitles an EC resident to free or reduced cost emergency medical treatment while visiting other Member States.

Earned Income   The income that is realised or accrued within a given accounting period.

Earned Surplus   An accounting term referring to a surplus of earnings that results from an accumulation of profits.

EEC   (See European Economic Communities)

ECGD   (See Export Credits Guarantee Department)

Economic and Monetary Union (EMU)   The European Commission three-stage plan for a movement towards EC economic and monetary union which involves a common currency and a common monetary policy.

Economically Inactive Persons   A European Community term which refers to citizens living in a Member State other than their own who are by choice rather than necessity not gainfully employed, for example, retired people.

Economic Systems   The private enterprises which are privately owned and operated and public enterprises which are owned by the state and run by the government on behalf of the public community. The type of economy a country is said to have is based on the extent to which there is state intervention.

Market Economy – a market economy is based on the private ownership of the factors of production and limited intervention by the government.
Command Economy – in a command economy the state largely controls the factors of production and the means of exchange and distribution.
Mixed Economy – a mixed economy has a combination of elements taken from a free economy and some from a controlled economy, i.e. a mixture of public and private enterprise.

Economies of Scales   Economies of scale are the advantages gained by a large-scale organisation because of its size which results in unit costs falling as output increases. These advantages include:
• Bulk buying reduces costs
• Find it easier to raise or borrow capital
• More capital is available for:
  a) extensive advertising
  b) research and development
  c) employing specialist personnel
  d) purchase of labour-saving machinery.

There are two major divisions of economies of scale:

1) **Internal Economies** – arise due to the growth in production of the firm, for example:

Weekly output of teddy bears	Average cost (£)
100	1.00
200	.90
1000	.75

2) **External Economies** – arise due to a growth of the industry in which the firm operates.

ECU   (See European Currency Unit)

Edit   To change or improve information, for example, in a computer file or on a page.

EFTPOS   Electronic fund transfer at point of sale. The process whereby banks and retailers co-operate in the use of cards which automatically debit the consumer's account when purchases are made. The EC has recommended a voluntary Code of Practice for banks and retailers on use of cards in this manner. (See also Point of Sale Terminal)

Ego Bait   Advertisements aimed at flattering the target audience. By pandering to their egos the advertiser hopes to make them more receptive to the message.

Electronic Fund Transfer (EFT)   The method of transferring booking details and payment instructions along telephone wires and via satellites around the world to transfer money very quickly.

Electronic Mail   The process by which letters are sent by a computer along telephone lines to come up on a VDU or be printed out at their destination.

Embargo   A government ban (can be total or partial) by one country on trade with another country.

Embezzle   To convert (money or property entrusted to one) fraudulently to one's own use.

Employee   Someone who works for another in return for a wage payment.

Employer's Liability Insurance   A type of insurance which enables employers to make provision for employees to able to obtain compensation for injuries sustained in the course of work. There is a legal obligation for employers to provide this type of insurance.

Employment Protection Acts   A range of UK laws providing employees with statutory protection against unfair dismissal and with other rights.

Endorsement   To authorise something by signing your name on it. For example, a signature on the back of a cheque by the payee authorises transfer of ownership of the cheque to another person.

Endowment Policy   A life assurance policy where benefit is payable at an agreed date or at death if earlier.

Enterprise Zones   These are small geographical areas in the UK designated by the UK government. Enterprise zones are particularly identified in run-down inner-city areas where economic decay is a problem.

Entrepôt Trade   The import of foreign produced goods to be re-exported. Entrepôt Traders act like wholesalers, breaking bulk, and sending mixed cargoes to countries that are small users, i.e. too small to take a complete cargo of one commodity.

Entrepreneur   People who organise and co-ordinate the factors of production. They are the owners of business enterprises who, by providing products or services, taking risks and making decisions, hope to make a profit.

Enquiry   A letter or standard form that is sent by a prospective buyer to one or several firms seeking information about products or services available.

Environmental Labelling   A term which refers to the claims on the packaging by manufacturers of the environmental effect of their products, for example, that a product is ozone friendly. It is also referred to as Green Labelling.

Environmentally Sensitive Areas (ESAs)   Designated areas which are given grants to encourage farmers to follow traditional methods of agriculture and to avoid intensive farming. ESAs are part of the Common Agricultural Policy of the EC.

Equilibrium Price   When any two forces balance the equilibrium price is where the quantity consumers want to buy is matched exactly by the quantity producers are willing to offer for sale.

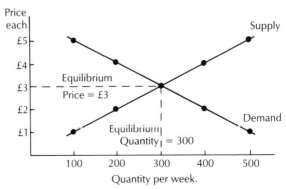

Price	Quantity demanded	Quantity supplied
£5	100	500
£4	200	400
£3	300	300
£2	400	200
£1	500	100

Equities   Ordinary shares. They represent a share in the ownership of a company. Each share is entitled to an equal proportion (dividend) of the company's profits.

Ergonomics   The study of the relationship between workers and their environment with the aim of designing tools, machines and the working environment to make the most effective use of labour.

ERM   (See European Monetary System)

Escalator Clause   A clause in a contract which stipulates an adjustment in price, wages, etc., in the event of specified changes in conditions, for example, large rise in cost of raw materials or in the cost of living.

Escape Clause   A clause included in a contract allowing the release of one or more of the parties if certain events occur.

Escrow   Money, goods, or a written document, such as a contract or bond, delivered to a third party and held by him pending the fulfilment of some condition.

ESPRIT   European Strategic Programme for Research and Development in Information Technology. A major co-operation, research and development project of the EC involving businesses, colleges and research organisations.

Estate Agent   A person who acts on behalf of another in the selling, buying or renting of property.

Estimate   To form an approximate idea of the expected cost of the supply of goods or services when it is not possible to provide an accurate cost. It is determined on the basis of current information and is in advance of actual production or servicing and, therefore, cannot be considered as precise.

Estoppel   A legal term meaning that an individual is precluded from denying a statement that he has previously made.

ETA   Estimated time of arrival.

ETD   Estimated time of departure.

EUREKA   An initiative to promote collaborative research in nonmilitary technology between companies from many countries, including the Member States of the EC.

Eurobonds   Bonds issued by governments or large international companies where the investor must be an owner of foreign currency outside the country of the currency's origin.

Eurocheque   A facility whereby a holder of a cheque card can cash his cheque at a large number of banks in Europe and other parts of the world

Eurodollar   US dollars as part of a European holding. They are used as a means of short or medium-term finance, especially in international trade, because of their easy convertability.

European Atomic Energy Authority (EURATOM)   The body established within the EC to promote the development of nuclear energy for peaceful purposes.

European Communities (EC)   The collective name for the European Economic Community, the European Coal and Steel Community and the European Atomic Energy Community.

European Court of Justice   The Court of Justice of the European Communities ensures that EC law is observed. See pages 78–9.

European Currency Unit (ECU)   The basic monetary unit used in EC transactions. The rate of the ECU against the national currencies is calculated daily by the Commission. Its value is calculated against a 'basket' of EC currencies.

European Economic Community (EEC)   The official name for the Common Market which is the economic association of European countries; today it is commonly referred to just as The European Community. The Community aims to promote a common market in goods and services and free movement of labour and capital and a common agricultural policy. The main institutions involved in the running of the European Community are:

- **The Council of Ministers** – this is the Community's principal decision-making body. The government of each Member nation in the Community has a seat on the Council. The Foreign Minister is usually the country's main representative, but a government is free to send any of its ministers to the Council meetings.
- **The Commission** – this is the guardian of the treaties that set up the European Community and is responsible for ensuring that the treaties are implemented.

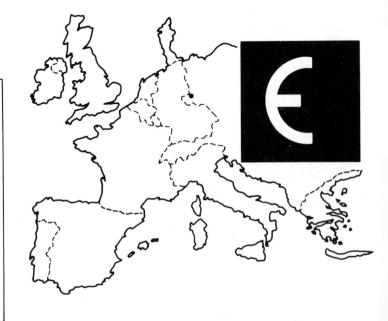

Members

Belgium
Denmark
France
Germany
Greece
Ireland
Italy
Luxembourg
Netherlands
Portugal
Spain
United Kingdom

Population
320 million

The European Parliament

1   Advises the Council of Ministers on Commission proposals
2   With the Council of Ministers, determines the Community budget
3   Exerts some political control over the Council and Commission

The Court of Justice

Settles legal disputes involving Community

The Structure of the European Community

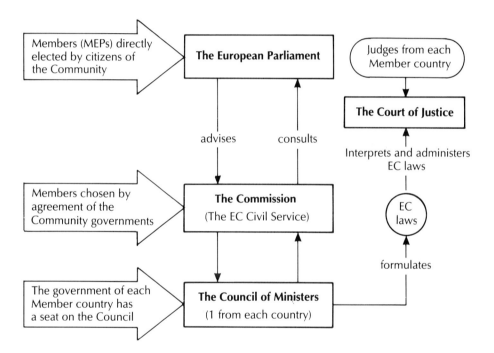

The Aim of the European Community
To establish a peaceful and prosperous Europe and to develop close economic and political co-operation

Members (MEPs) directly elected by citizens of the Community

The European Parliament

Judges from each Member country

The Court of Justice

advises   consults

Interprets and administers EC laws

Members chosen by agreement of the Community governments

The Commission
(The EC Civil Service)

EC laws

The government of each Member country has a seat on the Council

The Council of Ministers
(1 from each country)

formulates

The Council of Ministers

The Community's principal decision-making body

The Commission

1   Proposes Community policy
2   Responsible for administration of the Community

- **The European Parliament (EP)** – this consists of members (Members of the European Parliament – MEP) who represent the citizens of the European Community. They are elected by the electorate of their own country. The function of the EP is to advise the Council of Ministers on Commission proposals, determine the budget for the Community (with the Council of Ministers), and it exerts some political control over the Council and the Commission.
- **The European Court of Justice** – this settles legal disputes involving Community laws. The Court consists of judges from each Community country.

European Free Trade Association (EFTA)   An economic free trade area created in 1960 providing free trade in industrial goods between a number of European countries. The UK was once a member of EFTA but left to join the EEC. The two trading blocs recently sealed a deal effectively creating a 19-nation economic zone which comes into force in 1993.

Euromarket (or Euromart)   Alternative names for the Common Market.

European Monetary System (EMS)   The monetary system set up by the EC to stabilise exchange rates between European currencies. The elements of EMS are:

- **The European Currency Unit (ECU)** – the basic monetary unit used in Community transactions. Its value is established from the average 'basket' of EC currencies.
- **The Exchange Rate Mechanism (ERM)** – Member States which participate in the ERM system keep the value of their currencies within an agreed band in relation to the ECU.

European Regional Development Fund (ERDF)   Part of the EC's budget intended to help less developed areas of the Community and those suffering from economic decline and high unemployment.

Europoort   A port in the Netherlands (near Rotterdam) developed in the 1960s to meet increase in EC trade. There are now several other ports that have developed similarly to meet EC demand.

Eurovision   The network of the European Broadcasting Union providing exchange of news and television programmes amongst its member organisations and for the relay of news and programmes from outside the network.

Examination   A term used in accounting to refer to an examination of the accounts of a business – a financial examination.

Examination of Title   An examination carried out by a solicitor, to ensure that ownership of property, usually land, truly belongs to the person offering it as security to support borrowing.

Excess   An amount of money which an insurance policy may require someone to pay towards the cost of each claim made.

Exchange   1) Special market place where merchants and dealers may meet to do business.   2) To hand over or transfer goods in return for the equivalent value in kind rather than in money (e.g. barter).

Exchange Commission   A banking term referring to a charge made for exchanging one currency into another.

Exchange Control   The restriction of the movement of currency across national frontiers.

Exchange Control Form   A form needed for trade with countries which impose foreign exchange controls. Without this form, the remittance of money may be disallowed.

Exchange Equilisation Account   The account at the Bank of England in which the UK's gold and currency reserves are held. The managers of the account have the task of ensuring that the price of the pound in terms of other currencies is maintained at the level the Treasury wants it to be.

Exchange Rate Mechanism (ERM)   (See European Monetary System)

Exchange Rates   The rates at which one currency will be exchanged for another.

Excise Duties   The duties on certain goods, including petrol, alcohol and tobacco. The EC would like to make the rate of duty similar for all Member States in due course.

Exclusive Distribution Agreements   The agreements by a party to deal only with one other party in a given territory. In Europe such agreements are subject to the Community's competition rules.

Executor   A person appointed under the terms of a Will to carry out the wishes of the testator (the person to whom the Will refers).

Exempt Agreement   A consumer credit agreement where a creditor (e.g. a building society) finances the purchase of land, where repayment is in not more than four instalments or where the charge for credit does not exceed a supply.

Expected Life   The expected value likely to be derived from an asset or group of assets of a business.

Expenses   All costs that have to be met by a business that are deductable from income/revenue. If expenses exceed revenues, there is a loss; if revenues exceed expenses, there is a profit.

Export Credits Guarantee Department (ECGD)   The section of the UK Department of Trade which plays an important part in helping exporters by providing the following on a non-profit basis:

1) Insurance against non-payment of debts by foreign importers due to:
   a) Importer being unable to pay.
   b) Export restrictions by the UK government.
   c) Political restraints (for example, war or diplomatic relations) on payment.
2) Grants or low interest loans to assist exporters in meeting initial expense of exporting.

Exporter   A trader who sells goods abroad.

Export House   A business that undertakes the sale, distribution and delivery to the overseas customer, and assumes the financial risk involved in obtaining payment.

Export Invoice   A summary of invoices. It is issued to an importer by an agent in the country where the goods are bought.

Export Licence   A licence required for some specified categories of goods before they can be exported, for example, military weapons and some historical artefacts. In the case of military weapons the control is required to prevent sales to potential enemies. The sale of items of historical importance are restricted to preserve national heritage.

Exports   Goods that are sent abroad and result in foreign currency being brought into the exporting country.

Express Post   A special postal service provided by the UK Post Office which enables letters and parcels up to a certain size and weight to be accepted for delivery by special messenger. The word EXPRESS must be shown clearly in the top left hand corner of the package.

Ex Ship A quotation of the selling price of goods which includes their cost of transportation until they are unloaded from the ship at the destination port.

External Audit An examination of a company's accounts by a person who is not an employee of the organisation being investigated.

Extractive Industries The primary producers who are involved with the extraction of basic materials provided by nature, which are either on or below the earth's surface. The extractive industries are farming, fishing and mining. Without these much subsequent production would not take place.

Extraordinary Loss A loss which has occurred that is so unusual that it receives special treatment in the accounting process by a separate disclosure.

Ex Works A price quotation of goods that includes packing but not transport. It is also sometimes referred to as ex-warehouse

Face Amount The nominal amount of a mortgage, note, bond, etc., that is exclusive of interest or dividend accumulations.

Facility Letter A letter addressed to a borrowing customer from a bank specifying the terms and amount of a borrowing facility.

Facsimile An exact copy or reproduction.

Fascimile Signature A stamped or printed signature which is a copy of an original signature. It is used by businesses who issue large quantities of cheques or other important signed documents. Where such a signature is used in respect of cheque issues, the format must be agreed with the bank before putting into effect.

Facsimile Transmission A telecommunications facility which enables exact copies of documents, drawings and photographs to be transmitted by electronic signals from one site to another, both at home and overseas.

Factor A middleman or agent who sells goods or services on behalf of others but deals in his own name and actually has the goods in his possession. He sells and delivers the goods to the buyer and renders an account to his principal, less a commission charge.

Factor Price The price at which a producer sells to a wholesaler.

Factoring Debts   A service provided by a factoring company of collecting and guaranteeing payment of debts, thus releasing the businessman of the need to worry about debt collection. The factor takes over the sales invoices of a company, paying them immediately, less a commission, and collects the full amount outstanding in due course.

Factors of Production   The resources which form the basis for all business activity, land, labour, and capital. Entrepreneurship is sometimes referred to as a separate fourth factor of production although this is also a part of labour.

Can you identify the factors of production shown in this illustration?

Factories Act   An Act of the UK Parliament which covers factories and also includes brickworks, cement works, construction sites, dry cleaners, garages, gas works, laundries, potteries and many other work places where mechanical machinery is used. The Act includes the following rules:

- Work places must be properly lit and well ventilated
- Sufficient toilet and washing facilities must be provided
- Moving machinery must have a fenced surround
- Hoists, lifts, etc must be properly constructed and maintained
- Floors, passages and stairs must be kept unobstructed

• Floors must not have slippery surfaces
• Fire escapes must be provided and maintained.

Fair Market Value An estimate of the worth of a product or service in the absence of a specific quoted value.

Fair Trading Act 1973 An Act of the UK Parliament which established a permanent Office of Fair Trading. This is a government body with the broad function to keep watch on trading matters in the UK and protect both consumers and business people against unfair practices.

Family Protection Policy An assurance policy which provides for an annuity to be paid, usually to the widow, if the life assured dies. It is the sort of cover that a family man might take out to provide for his family in the case of premature death. Such a policy is usually taken out for a limited period, for example, until the children are old enough to look after themselves.

Fast Food Quickly-prepared food sold in an eatable form with minimal waiting time for the customer during preparation. Fast food may be consumed on or off the seller's premises.

Fate of a Cheque A banking term that means to enquire if a cheque has been paid or dishonoured.

Feasability Study A study carried out by experts before a decision is taken to follow a particular course of action.

Federalist Someone who supports the ideal of an eventual United States of Europe with a single European government.

Feedback The final stage in communication when the receivers show whether they have understood or acted on the message sent.

Ficticious Asset An asset which arises because of expenditure on non-visible items. Because they do not have a realisable value they are deducted from the capital figure of a company's accounts, for example, goodwill.

Fiduciary One who acts on behalf of another in financial matters following written authority and is responsible for the assets managed.

Fiduciary Issue Notes and coins issued by the central bank of a country backed only by the securities of the Government (for example, not backed by gold).

Field Auditor   An internal auditor whose function is to examine the accounts of branches or plants located away from the principle office.

FIFO   The abbreviation of First In First Out. A system of costing stock and production materials. As stock is used it is normally expected that stock that was purchased first will be sold before more recently purchased stock. Valuation of stock is based on this assumption. (See also LIFO)

Filing   Putting documents or information into a system of order so that they can quickly be retrieved at some time in the future. The system may be a manual or a computerised one. There are a variety of ways of classifying items in a filing system but the main methods are, alphabetical, numerical, geographical, subject and chronological. Sometimes combinations of these are employed, for example, alpha-numerical:

- **Alphabetical** – items are filed alphabetically, like the words in a dictionary or names in a telephone directory.
- **Numerical** – documents or files are given a number and then placed in numerical order.
- **Geographical** – in this system items are filed alphabetically according to their place of origin, for example, town or country.
- **Subject** – items are placed in alphabetical order under topic headings rather than by the name of correspondents.
- **Chronological** – this means placing items in date order.

Finance   Provision of money for commercial or government undertakings.

Finance Company (Finance House)   Businesses which are mainly involved in lending money to finance hire purchase and other credit transactions.

Finance Costs   Expenditures related to the process of supplying money or credit necessary to conduct the operations of business activities.

Finance House Base Rate   A fluctuating rate based upon the three month interbank rate and averaged according to a set formula over an eight week period.

Finance Lease   A lease where the lessor supplies the finance but has no commercial interest in the equipment. The rental paid by the lessee will cover the cost of equipment, interest and profit.

Financial Statement A balance sheet or similar statement which supports accounting information derived from accounts records.

Financial Times Index (FT INDEX) Indexes published in the Financial Times newspaper showing movements of UK securities. The most well known is the FT Industrial Ordinary Share Index which is based on the prices of 30 major shares which are held to represent a measure of the market as a whole. It is this particular index that is known as the FT Index or 'Footsie'.

Fine Rate The lowest or most favourable rate of interest that is charged to first-class borrowers.

Fire Insurance An insurance which provides cover against loss as a result of fire lightning and explosions.

Firm A commercial enterprise.

Firm Offer A definite offer to purchase specific property at a stated price.

Fiscal Policy The government's policy for raising revenue (for example, by taxation) and spending (for example, the Armed Services).

Fiscal Year An accounting period of 12 months, which may or may not correspond with the calendar year. At the end of this period, during which financial records are maintained, the accounts are closed and summarised in a financial statement.

Fixed Assets Assets such as plant, machinery, and fittings that are used many times over and are necessary to enable a business to operate and remain trading.

Fixed Charge 1) In accounting a fixed charge has to be met regularly irrespective of the amount of business transacted. 2) A liability which is redeemable against specific non-movable assets of a company (for example, property).

Fixed Charge Debenture A debenture which is guaranteed by a specific asset as collateral.

Fixed Costs Expenditures which do not change in total as the rate of output varies. For example, rent and depreciation are fixed costs.

Fixed Deposit A deposit with a financial institution, such as a bank, for a fixed period of time where the interest rate is also fixed for the full period.

Fixed Liability   (See Long-term Liability)

Fixed Loans   Usually long-term loans taken out for a fixed period. A fixed rate of interest is charged depending upon amount borrowed and the length of the repayment period. Repayment is generally on a monthly basis.

Flexible Working Time (FWT, Flexitime)   All the names given to a system of arranging working hours so that at 'peak' or 'core' times all members of staff are at work. Outside core time employees are allowed to choose the hours they work, so long as they complete the required number of hours in the week.

The working day of the firm is commonly defined in three ways:

1) **Band time** – the total period of time the business operates, for example, 8.00 am to 6.00 pm.
2) **Core time** – the period of time when all members of the firm are expected to be at work, for example, 11.00 a.m. to 2.00 p.m.
3) **Flexible time** – the period outside core time when employees can choose whether they work or not, so long as they complete the total number of hours they are paid for.

To choose their working hours employees first calculate core time. Core time in the example below is 5 days × 3 hours (11.00 a.m to 2.00 p.m.) = 15 hours. This leaves 20 hours (35 − 15 = 20) of working which can be chosen from FWT. Before choosing the hours of flexitime, employees will have to take into account the time they wish to use for lunch breaks. Most firms will insist that the employee takes at least a 30 minute lunch break.

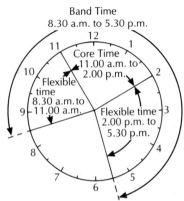

Band Time
8.30 a.m. to 5.30 p.m.

Total hours to be worked by employee = 35 hours

Float   A cash advance to cover anticipated expenditure until such time as these costs are repaid.

Floating Charge   A floating charge is one that is secured against the circulating assets of a company (i.e. against debtors, stock, plant and machinery).

Floating Charge Debenture   A debenture which is guaranteed by collateral not of a fixed nature.

Floppy Disk   A flexible computer disk used to store programs and data.

Flow Charts   Diagrams used to break a task or sequence of operations down into smaller parts.

Fluctuation   To rise and fall; change. For example, the price of purchasing a foreign currency goes up and down in relation to the supply and demand.

FOB   (See Free on Board)

Folio   A referring item such as a page number or voucher number in an accounting sub-system such as petty cash records. The folio indicates the source of an accounting entry.

Food Aid   Food made available by the European Community and other bodies for aid to less-developed countries experiencing food shortages due to natural or other disasters. Some surpluses are also distributed for hardship relief schemes within the EC.

Food and Drugs Act 1955   An Act of the UK Parliament which is enforced by local government health inspectors. It helps to protect consumers because it:

● Forbids the sale of unfit food.
● States hygienic conditions for production and sale of food products.
● Regulates labelling and description of items.
● Provides minimum standards in food composition (for example, the meat content of sausages etc.).

For Cash   A Stock Exchange term, but often used for other circumstances, which means that settlement must be made at the time the deal is transacted.

Force   The EC programme for the development of continuing vocational education.

Foreclose   To take possession of property put up as collateral when an outstanding debt has not been repaid.

Foreign Trade   Trade with firms based in another country:

- **Exporting** – selling to another country
- **Importing** – buying from another country.

Foreign Currency Securities   Securities which are expressed in a foreign currency and where interest or dividends are paid in that currency.

Foreign Draft   A draft payable abroad and drawn in a foreign currency.

Foreign Exchange   The exchange of one currency for another at shifting market prices.

Forfeit   To have taken away, perhaps because of some default or crime.

Forged Signature   When a bank pays a cheque bearing a forged signature the amount concerned cannot be debited to the customer's account, even if the forgery appears indistinguishable from the genuine signature.

Forgery   A false writing with deliberate intent to defraud others.

Forward Deal   A contract for a purchase or sale at an agreed price at a future date, for example, in three months time. (See Spot Deal and Futures Deal)

Forward Exchange   The purchase or sale of foreign currency for delivery at a future date.

Forwarding Instructions   Instructions given by a shipper to his suppliers telling them where and when to forward the goods.

Forward Rate   The rate at which foreign exchange can be bought or sold under a foreign exchange contract. This is usually at a more favourable rate of exchange than that currently operating, but may be adversely affected by future rate fluctuations.

Founder's Shares (Deferred Shares)   These are company shares usually granted to the founders of the firm as part payment when a company has been bought. They usually carry voting rights, but give rights to a share of the company profits only after the ordinary shareholders have received a dividend.

Franchising The permission given by a company to someone to buy the right to use their products or techniques under their trade name. Franchising offers a 'ready made' business opportunity for those with sufficient capital and a willingness to work hard. The franchisee pays for the name, products, or services of the franchiser who receives a lump sum and a share of the profits of the business. The franchisee receives the majority of the profits, but must also meet most of the losses. In return for the money they receive, in addition to allowing use of their name, products, techniques, or services, franchisers usually provide an extensive marketing back-up.

Franco A quotation of the selling price of goods in the buyer's currency which includes all transportation costs up to the point where the goods are delivered to the buyer's premises.

Franking Machine Machines which are bought or hired from firms licensed by the UK Post Office. The hirer pays for units of postage value which are held in the machine's meter. The machine is used to print the postage paid on envelopes and parcel labels. As postage is used up the meter reading changes and eventually has to be replenished. A slogan can be printed at the same time as the postage paid to advertise company profits.

A postal franking includes a space that can be used to print an advertising slogan or a return address in a distinctive colour.

Fraud   The practice of deception with the intention of cheating another person.

Fraudulent Conveyance   The situation in which a debtor, in an attempt to defeat or delay paying his creditors, transfers property. This transaction can be held as void and transferee can be required to return the property to the trustee in bankruptcy.

Free Alongside Ship (FAS)   A quotation of the selling price of goods which includes their cost of transportation to a specified ship at the port of departure.

Freefone   Operator-connected calls on a transferred charge basis, used by businesses that wish to allow their customers or agents to make telephone calls to them without payment, thus encouraging custom.

Freehold   The right to hold and dispose of land with the full right of ownership.

Freeholder   The possessor of freehold estate.

Free Movement   The ability of people, goods, services and capital to move freely between the Member States of the EC, without physical, legal, technical or other barriers between them.

Free on Board (F.O.B.)   A price quotation of goods for export which includes all costs (for example, packing and transportation) to the point where the goods are loaded on to a specified ship.

Free on Rail (or Truck)   A quotation of the selling price of goods including their handling charges until the goods are load onto a train at the nearest station (or on to a truck).

Freeport   A port, or section of a port, which is considered to be outside the customs frontier of the country in which it is situated. The idea behind a freeport is to allow facilities whereby goods can enter the area duty free, be worked on in some way, and then exported free of duty.

Freepost   A service in the UK which allows people to write to traders in reply to advertisements without paying postage, as long as the envelope is addressed in a particular way.

• The address must include the word FREEPOST.
• Only the second-class service is available.
• The trader is saved the expense of providing envelopes.

Free Trade   Trade which is not hindered by protectionist measures or policies.

Freightliner   British Rail's high speed container service which links up with special road and sea terminals.

Freight Note   The bill or charge for shipping goods. It is sent by the exporter to the shipping company.

Frictional Unemployment   Unemployment caused by temporary readjustments between the supply of and demand for labour. The problem can be met by increasing the mobility of labour or ensuring that the labour supply has the appropriate skills needed, for example, increased scientific and technical skills.

Fringe Benefits   Invisible additions to the wages of employees, and are sometimes referred to as 'perks'. Some examples are free or subsidised meals, company car, free private health and pensions, low interest loans, etc.

Fund   An asset or group of assets that is set aside for specific uses, such as a petty cash fund, or a working fund.

Funding   Where a borrower makes arrangements with his banker to transfer his overdraft to a loan repayable by regular instalments, for example.

Future Costs   Costs expected to be incurred at a later date.

Futures Deal   A contract to buy or sell something where the date of the transaction is in the future but other details, such as price, quantity, quality, etc., are agreed at the time of contract.

Futures Market (or Terminal Trading)   A market where contracts are agreed for delivery at a future date, for example, a fixed quantity of a raw material or crop.

FWD   An abbreviation for carried forward. This term is used to indicate that certain columnar totals are carried forward to a new page, or that the beginning figures of a column were carried forward from the preceding page.

Gain   The excess of revenue over related costs.

Gearing   The relationship between the various sources of a company's finance, i.e. between a company's borrowings (permanent loan capital – preference shares and debentures) and its equity capital (ordinary shares). It is correctly referred to as capital gearing and is usually expressed as a ratio. A business is highly geared if the proportion of borrowed money is high in relation to shareholders funds or net worth and low when the opposite applies.

General Agreement on Tariffs and Trade (GATT)   An international organisation set up in 1947 which now has over 80 member nations that seek to increase the volume of international trade by reducing trade restrictions (for example, quotas and tariffs).

General Average   A loss intentionally incurred in order to preserve the interests of all, for example, to jettison of some cargo to lighten a ship in difficulty at sea. The cost of the loss incurred is shared by all parties, usually through insurance cover.

General Meeting   A meeting that may be attended by all the shareholders of a company.

General Overhead   A classification of expense used in accountancy which is used to identify costs that cannot be directly associated with the development of a product or the rendering of a service. Also referred to as general expense.

General Partner   A person who, either alone or with others, is liable for the debts of the partnership. (See also Sleeping Partner)

General Union   A union that accepts members from a wide range of occupations, for example, Transport and General Workers Union.

Geographical Mobility   A term used to describe the movement of a factor of production from one area to another area within a region, within a country, or between countries.

Giffen Goods   A name given to those essential and relatively cheap goods for which demand is likely to increase following a rise in price. The term Giffen' is given in recognition of a nineteenth century economist of that name who noticed that when the price of bread increased, consumers bought more of it, being unable to buy more expensive alternatives.

Gilt Edged (Gilts)   Securities of the highest class which are readily realisable (turned into cash), for example, UK government stock.

Giro   A system of making payments to others by credit transfer. In the UK there is the bank giro system, and also the National Girobank system which operates through the Post Office.

Glut   The excess of supply over demand, often leading to a fall in price.

Going Concern   A business that is in operation and is expected to continue to trade profitably.

Golden Triangle   The central region of the EC which is expected to see the greater proportion of economic growth after 1992. The area is subject to many 'guestimates' but typical vertices might be Bristol, Hanover and Milan.

Gone Concern   An attempt to measure the value of a business assuming the worst conditions, for example, assuming that it is about to fail. Each asset is valued in an attempt to evaluate what proceeds would be available for the creditors of the business.

Good Faith   To act honestly. In the case of insurance, to honestly declare all known information. In the case of a cheque, to take it in good faith means to take it assuming that the presenter is the rightful owner.

Goods in Process   1) An item in production that is partially complete.   2) Raw material which has been processed to some part degree, for example, fruit that has been cooked and is waiting to be canned.

Goods Returned Note   A document sent with goods being returned to the supplier.

Goodwill   The public opinion of a business which can be recognised as an advantage that the firm would have over a new similar business being established. Goodwill is the good relationship that the firm has established with its customers, and is often shown as an asset if the firm is valued for sale.

Go-slow   A form of industrial action whereby workers do their job but deliberately slacken the pace of production.

Government Securities   Treasury bills and funded stocks.

Grade   An agreed classification of certain types of goods into scale, rank, or size.

Gratuity (Tip)   A voluntary payment made in addition to the actual cost of a service provided, for example, a tip to a lorry driver for making prompt delivery.

Green Card   A document provided by a driver's insurance company which shows that a driver's comprehensive insurance has been extended to cover motoring in other countries.

Green Curency   The EC Common Agricultural Policy guarantees prices, fixed in European Currency Units (ECUs), to farmers for their products. Green currency is the name given for the system used to convert these CAP support prices into national currencies.

Grievance Procedure   The stages followed in an attempt to solve a dispute between a worker and their employer.

Gross   The total amount of money or goods without any deductions.

Gross Domestic Product (GDP)   The total value of output produced within a country in a specified period of time.

Examples of UK GDP (average measure – 1985 = 100)

1969	1979	1988	1989
260.1	331.0	404.4	413.3 (£ million)

Gross Interest   Interest earned on an investment which is received before deduction of tax.

Gross National Product (GNP)   The total value of goods and services produced by the residents of a country within a specified period of time. This includes the income of residents from property and investments abroad (unlike GDP which does not include foreign earnings).

Gross Profit   The difference between total revenue from sales and the total cost of purchases or materials without deduction of indirect costs. It is usually expressed as a percentage and calculated in the following way:

$$\text{Gross profit percentage} = \frac{\text{Gross profit}}{\text{Turnover}} \times 100$$

Gross Sales (Gross Revenue)   The total revenue from sales but after deducting the value of discounts and other expenses directly related to the transaction.

Gross Up   To increase income to its pre-tax value.

Gross Weight   The total weight of an article, inclusive of the weight of the packing or container.

Gross Yield   The return received on an investment prior to the payment of any taxes.

Growth Stock   A share which is expected to appreciate in capital value rather than provide a high yield.

Guarantee   A promise given by the producers of goods to make good any defects in their products within a specified period of time from the date of purchase.

Guarantor   A person who undertakes to accept responsibility for the debts of another should that person default.

Guardian   A legal representative of a person too young to handle their own financial affairs.

Hammering   An announcement of the failure of a Stock Exchange firm.

Hansard   The official printed reports of debates and proceedings in the UK Houses of Parliament.

Hardcopy   Computer output printed on paper.

Hardware   The physical components of a computer system such as its monitor, systems unit, keyboard and printer.

Hawkers   Traders, generally dealing in small items or services, and using some form of transport to take their wares (for example, greengrocery) direct to the customer's door for their convenience. In the UK such traders require a licence from the local Council in order to trade in this manner.

Health and Safety at Work Act 1974   An Act of the UK Parliament which sets out the duties of both the employer and the employee relating to health and safety in the workplace.

• The employer's duty can be summed up as the responsibility to provide a safe workplace, including arrangements for hazards such as fire, and the maintenance of machinery and equipment.
• Employees also have the duty to take reasonable care for the safety of

themselves and other working colleagues at all times, and to cooperate with the employer on all matters of safety.

Health, Department of   This government department is responsible for the National Health Service in the UK , and the local authority operated welfare services run for the elderly, the infirm, and the handicapped.

Hedging   The name given to the process used, particularly in the futures market, to cancel out price fluctuations. For example, a producer may use the system to ensure a guaranteed price of raw materials. The method employed is to make two contracts:

1) One contract is made to obtain goods to purchase, or to dispose of goods to be sold.
2) A second contract is made whereby the 'hedger' either;
   a) Makes a profit that will offset any loss caused by price movements against them, or
   b) Foregoes a profit they might have made as a result of prices moving in their favour.

HGV   Heavy goods vehicle.

Hidden Reserve   An accounting term that is used to describe a reserve of money that a company holds but is not included in its accounts. Such a reserve is 'created' (illegally) by showing the value of some assets as lower than their true value.

High Coupon   A name sometimes given to a share or stock yielding a high rate of interest or return.

Hire   1) To acquire the temporary use of something, or the services of a person in exchange for a payment.   2) To provide the use of something, or a person's or firm's services in exchange for a payment.

Hire Purchase   A contract for hiring goods for a fixed period with an option to purchase them for a nominal sum (for example, £1) at the end of the period. An initial deposit may be paid, which consists of a percentage of the purchase price, and a number of equal weekly or monthly instalments are repaid over a given period. Interest is charged for the credit given. The goods do not become the property of the buyer until the last instalment has been paid. The item must not be sold until the last repayment has been made because the finance company remains the rightful owner until then. The seller can repossess the item if the buyer defaults on repayments. But there are some restrictions on repossession laid down in the UK by the Consumer Credit Act, 1974:

- If the buyer has paid one third of the value a court order is needed to repossess the item.
- The item cannot be repossessed at all once two-thirds of the value has been paid.

Histogram An illustrative representation of statistics in which the values or proportions are shown by a series of bars or rectangles.

Historical Cost The cost measured by actual payment of cash or its equivalent at the time of outlay. This is the cost to the present owner at the time of purchase and might be very different from the current value due to inflation for example.

Hire-Retailing Retail businesses engaged in renting out equipment to be used in the hirer's own home or place of work, for example, cement mixers, carpet cleaners, etc.

Holder The payee or endorsee of a bill or cheque who is in possession of it, or is the bearer of it.

Holder for Value The holder of a bill of exchange who has given value for it, or who is in possession of a bill for which value has been given.

Holder in due Course The holder of a bill of exchange or cheque who has acquired it honestly and in good faith, for value, believing (and having no reason to doubt) that the person who gave it to them had the right to it.

Holding The term used to describe the possession of a number of shares in one or more companies.

Holding Company A partnership of two or more businesses combined together to achieve a certain aim, for example, to bring together several processes into one production unit. This kind of partnership is usually incorporated as a holding company. Each member company retains its legal entity, but overall control lies with the holding company.

Holding Deed A deed which transfers the ownership of land to a new owner.

Home Trade The trade in goods and services within the home country.

Honour   To accept and meet an obligation. For example, to honour a cheque is to pay the amount due.

Honorary   A position or title held or given without salary or fee being paid.

Honorarium   A fee paid for a nominally free service.

Horizontal Integration/Horizontal Merger   Where firms engaged in similar activities combine forces to obtain production or marketing advantages.

Host Country   The country in which a person works or where a company operates, but which is not their 'home' country . In the case of a London business with a branch in Munich, the host country is Germany whereas the home country is England

Hot Card   A credit or cheque card which has been lost or stolen and which is being, or expected to be used fraudulently.

Hot Money   Capital transferred suddenly from one commercial centre to another (for example, from one country to another) seeking the highest interest rates or the best opportunity for a short-term gain.

House   A name sometimes given to a business organisation engaged in certain classes of activity.

House Advertising   Advertising which aims to promote or improve the image of a company as opposed to advertising the goods or services it offers.

House Magazine   A journal published by a business for circulation among its employees or shareholders.

House Union   A trade union whose members are only employed in a single firm.

Hovercraft   A vehicle that is able to travel across both land and water on a cushion of air. The cushion is produced by a fan or a peripheral of nozzles.

Hoverport   A port for hovercraft.

Hypermarket   A huge self-service store, usually built on the outskirts of a town.

Hypothecation   To pledge personal property as security for a debt without transferring possession or title to the lender.

Idle Capacity The unused production potential of a plant, machine, or operation.

Immigration To enter a country of which one is not a native in order to settle there.

Imperfect Competition The situation whereby goods are produced or marketed under conditions of near monopoly (i.e. no other supplier provides an identical item).

Implied Terms The terms of a contract which, although not actually stated in writing, can be assumed to form an important part of it, for example, in an agreement to sell someone something it would be reasonable to assume that it is in good working order.

Imports 1) Goods or services bought from other countries and resulting in an outflow of currency from the importing country.
2) Goods which are received from abroad

Import Duty A tax charged on the import of goods into a country.

Importers Businesses involved in bringing foreign goods into a country.

Import Licence A document issued by a government authorising the import of goods without restriction. These documents are sometimes called 'quota licences' because they restrict total imports to a given quota set by the government.

Import Quotas A quota is a limit placed by a government on the quantity of a product allowed to enter the country during a year. An import licence must be obtained before goods subject to quota restrictions can be imported.

Imprest Cash Petty cash that is maintained for miscellaneous expenses and is periodically reimbursed to a constant level.

Imprest System A simple accounting system for controlling petty cash expenses. A set amount of money is allocated as a 'float' from which sums are used for small payments as required and petty cash vouchers, bills, or receipts are used to record these expenditures. The float is regularly restored to its original level (the imprest) by the cashier presenting a summary account to the cashier. See the following page.

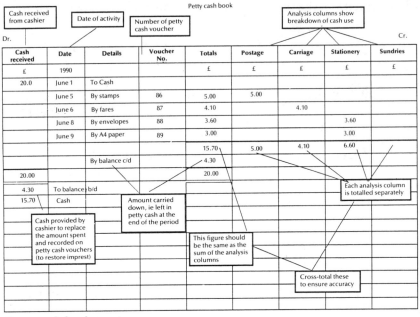

Petty cash book entries

Impluse Buying Purchases made on the spur of the moment without full consideration of the money available or how long it is required to last. Certain products such as ice cream and confectionery are not usually planned purchases.

Imputed Costs Costs that do not involve at any time actual cash outlay and which do not, therefore, appear in the financial records of a business.

Income The amount of monetary or other returns, either earned or unearned, received from work, business activity, investments, etc., over a period of time.

Income Tax A personal tax, usually progressive, levied on annual income subject to certain deductions, but in the UK generally deducted from each wage payment through the PAYE (Pay As You Earn) system.

Increment An increase in value over a specified period of time, for example, an increase in wages or salary on an annual basis.

Incremental Cost A change in cost that reflects the addition or subtraction of a unit of output.

Incumbrance A liability such as a mortgage upon a property.

Incur To become liable for, for example, a cost, expense, or loss.

Indemnifier A person who agrees to make good any loss or injury which is suffered.

Indemnity A term used in insurance and banking which refers to an arrangement whereby one party to a contract agrees to make good any loss or damage suffered by another to the extent that they are no worse off than they were before. They cannot profit from the event that has taken place but are only expected to recover the financial loss.

Indent An order received by an exporter from an overseas customer, giving them full instructions concerning the goods required, package markings wanted, shipping instructions, terms of sale, and method of payment.

Indenture An agreement between two or more persons that involves reciprocal rights and duties.

Independent Shops A type of shop owned by a sole trader (one shop) or an independent trader (less than ten branches). They tend to specialise in a narrow range of goods and operate on a small scale in comparison with multiples and supermarkets.

Index, Financial Times (See FT Index)

Index Linked Stock A type of UK government stock where the value of the principal and the interest are adjusted in line with changes in the cost of living index and adjusted accordingly. (See also RPI)

Index of Retail Prices (RPI) A statistical device used to measure changes in the prices of a representative selection of goods and services. The index is sometimes referred to as the cost of living index.

Indirect Cost A cost that is not readily identifiable with the production of specific goods or services but is applicable to the production activity in general. Overhead allocations for general and administrative activities are recognised as indirect costs.

Indirect Labour Labour that is not directly applicable to a product, such as the work of cleaners, security watchmen and other employees involved in general maintenance.

Indirect Liability The responsibility for the debt of another from which an obligation to pay may develop.

Indirect Material   Goods that are not an integral part of a product, such as materials that are needed for cleaning, oiling, and general maintenance.

Indirect Production   The production by specialisation whereby each worker contributes in part to the end product. Indirect production is an important feature of mass production – the system of making the greatest number of products with the least number of workers. (See also Division of Labour)

Indirect Tax   A tax levied on goods and services and collected (indirectly) for the government by other agencies such as retailers. VAT is an indirect tax, and so are Excise duties. By contrast, Income Tax is a direct tax.

Induction Course   A course run by an employer for new members of staff to help them to become familiar with the organisation and the work they are required to do and, therefore, to help them to become effective workers.

Industrial Action   Action taken, such as strike or go-slow, taken by workers in industry to protest against working conditions.

Industrial Life Assurance   Life assurance policies which are devised for people who find it difficult to raise an annual premium. The sum assured is generally small and premiums are collected weekly or monthly. These are generally policies without profits.

Industrial Relations   The relationship that exists between employers and their employees, or between the senior management of the organis-ation and the employees' representatives/trade unions.

Industrial Tribunal   A body appointed to adjudicate in disputes arising out of a person's employment such as claims for unfair dismissal, redundancy and equal pay.

Industrial Union   A union of workers from a single industry, for example, National Union of Mineworkers.

Industry   Organised economic activity concerned with manufacture, extraction and processing of raw materials or construction.

Industry, Location of   Sites where industries tend to be positioned. The following are typical of the factors which influence location of industry.

- **Industrial Inertia** – some firms tend to stay at a particular site even though the original reason for establishing in that area no longer applies
- **Site Facilities** – the site may be chosen because it gives ready access to required resources such as local sources of power, raw materials, mineral deposits, etc
- **Transport Influences** – siting near to good road, rail, sea, or air links can save in distribution costs or in the movement of raw materials
- **Market Pull** – there is a tendency for industries to locate near to their market because there are economic advantages to be gained.
- **Labour Supply** – industries need to locate within reach of their potential labour force.

Inertia Selling   The despatch of unsolicited goods to individuals in the hope that the goods will be purchased. This is now illegal in the UK.

Infant Industries   Industries at an early stage of development.

Inflation   The situation when prices in general are persistently rising causing the real value of money to decline. This means that the cost of living has increased as people's incomes are able to purchase less. Under such circumstances we say that real income has fallen, and this leads to a fall in the standard of living unless some factor changes. See the illustration on page 106. There are two broad types of inflation; cost-push inflation and demand-pull inflation.

- **Cost push Inflation** – this is caused by rises in the cost of the factors of production such as raw materials or labour, for example oil prices or wages. When such increased costs are passed on to the consumer in the form of increased prices this results in cost-push inflation. The resultant increase in the cost of living encourages workers to press for further wage increases causing a continuing inflationary spiral with rising wages chased by rising prices, or vice versa.
- **Demand pull Inflation** – this type of inflation involves 'too much money chasing too few goods', that is, an excessive supply of money relative to the goods and services available for purchase. Upward movement of wages can be an explanation of this, but 'too much money' usually refers to excessive credit expansion, for example, easier bank loans and hire purchase, etc., which encourages people to spend money that they do not immediately have available.

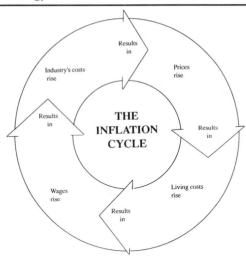

Information Technology The combined use of computers, communications and control systems, all based on digital electronic components, to process, store, disseminate and use vocal, pictorial, textual and numerical information.

Informative Advertising Advertising which tries to give people information about new products or about changes to old products without necessarily trying to influence them to buy.

Injunction An instruction or order issued by a Court to a party commanding something to be done or forbidding some activity.

Inland Mail The service provided by the UK Post Office which sends letters and parcels to destinations within the home country.

Inland Revenue A UK government board that administers and collects major direct taxes, such as Income Tax, Corporation Tax, and Capital Gains Tax.

Inland Waterways The rivers and canals used for inland transport of goods.

Innocent Misrepresentation An incorrect action made without the intention to deceive.

In Perpetuity For ever.

Input Information which is keyed into a computer or word processor.

Inscribed Stock Investment stocks which have the names of its purchasers kept in a central record as opposed to the alternative arrangement whereby each purchaser is given a certificate of ownership. For example, some UK Government Stock issued as part of National Savings are kept on a central register,

Insider Dealing The unfair and illegal use of special, 'price sensitive' knowledge of a company's affairs to make profitable bargains through The Stock Exchange.

Insolvent The situation where an individual, company, etc., have insufficient assets to meet debts and liabilities. A person who is insolvent is said to be bankrupt.

Inspection, Sale by The sale of goods in a manner whereby they are purchased from a display, for example, as in buying from a shop.

Issuing House An organisation involved in assisting in raising company finance by sponsoring issues of company shares on behalf of their clients, or acting as intermediaries between companies seeking capital and those willing to provide it. Merchant banks offer Issuing House facilities.

Instalment One of a number of payments towards an outstanding debt, for example, part of the repayment of a loan, or a credit sale agreement.

Instalment Credit A loan where repayment is made by regular, often monthly, instalments over an agreed period of time. Interest is calculated on the whole loan for the whole period and added to the amount before dividing it by the number of repayments to arrive at the amount of each instalment.

Institute An organisation founded to promote some public object, rule, law or principle, for example, Institute for European Environmental Policy (IEEP) – an independent, non-governmental organisation which undertakes analysis of environmental policies in Europe and promotes the development of EC policies which protect the environment.

Institutional Investor A person or company who collects and invests the savings of many others, for example, insurance companies, pension and union funds managers. (See also Pension Funds)

Instrument   A formal legal document that has a specific purpose, for example, a contract, cheque, bill of exchange, draft, etc.

Insurable Interest   A form of insurance which a person is allowed to buy if they would suffer a financial loss should the insured risk occur. In other words, they must have a genuine interest in the property or person insured. The interest need only exist at the time the insurance is effected. You can insure your garage but not that of your neighbour, unless you have insurable interest, for example, if your property is stored in your neighbour's garage.

Insurable Risks   Risks which insurance companies are willing to provide cover for. They must be due to an external event (i.e. not self-inflicted) and the probability of the risk must be capable of estimation.

Insurance   The provision of financial compensation in the event of a particular occurrence. It is a means of spreading the cost of large losses over a great number of those at risk so that no one individual bears the full cost of a loss. In return for a fee (the premium) insurance companies (the insurer) contracts (the policy) to indemnify/compensate the insured against losses incurred as a result of some specific event.

Insurance Agents   People who work for an insurance company or friendly society (specialists in life and sickness assurance), selling only the policies of that company.

Insurance Assessor/Adjustor   An independent person who adjusts losses fairly between the insurance company and and its policyholder.

Insurance/Assurance   The method by which people make arrangements to be paid money in the event of injury, death or loss, for example, property. Insurance is basically split into two different kinds:

- **Life Assurance** – by which you pay a regular premium to assure payment of an agreed cash sum whenever you die or when you reach a given age.
- **Non-Life Insurance** – gives you cover against something that may or may not happen

Insurance is not the same as assurance. Assurance makes for financial provision which comes into operation when something happens which you can guarantee will eventually happen. For example, you may assure yourself that you will receive a sum of money either when you reach the age of 60 or upon your death if you die before then. There is no uncertainty with assurance – you will either die or you will live to be 60.

Insurance Brokers   Independent professionals who sell insurance on a commission basis. Because they are independent, insurance brokers can sell the policies of a wide number of companies and, therefore, they are able to give unbiased advice as to which is the best policy for their customers to buy. Insurance brokers should not be confused with Lloyd's Brokers.

Insurance Brokers, Lloyd's   The source of contact with Lloyd's insurance market. By custom Lloyd's underwriters will not deal directly with the public. Potential clients with sufficient business to be of interest to underwriters put their business through a Lloyd's Broker. The function of Lloyd's Brokers is to get the best deal that they can for their clients, who may be large organisations such as businesses and local government.

Insurance Certificate   (See Insurance Policy)

Insurance Excess   An amount of money which an insurer may require a policyholder to pay towards the cost of each claim.

Insurance Market   The insurance market is the whole range of facilities through which people can purchase insurance cover. The UK insurance market is the largest in the world. The centre of the market is Lloyd's Corporation – often referred to as 'Lloyd's of London'. But the total market is far larger than just the central market, it includes insurance companies, agents, brokers, friendly societies, and Lloyd's Brokers. See page 110.

Insurance Policy   A document issued by the insurer to the insured giving details of the contract of insurance between them. The following documents may also be issued in association with the insurance policy:

- **Certificate of insurance** – for employers' liability and motor insurance, the law requires evidence of cover to be provided by this certificate
- **Cover note** – a temporary document provided whilst the certificate of insurance is being prepared
- **Endorsement** – a notice of an amendment to a policy, usually by the insurer. The endorsement is attached to the policy and thereafter becomes part of the contract

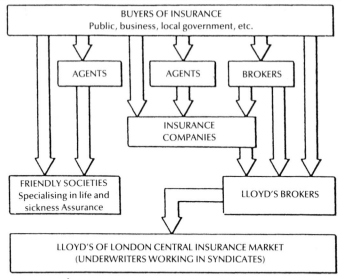

The insurance market

- **Renewal notice** – issued by the insurer prior to expiry date of policy, inviting the insured to renew the cover and advising the renewal premium and the date on which it is due.

Insurance Premium   The price charged by an insurance company for the cover given by the policy.

Insurance, Principles of   Four legal principles which, if honoured mean that insurance will work effectively and fairly for all those involved:

  1) **Insurable interest** – insurance cover can only be taken out by the person with insurable interest. A policyholder has an insurable interest if the insured event would involve them in financial loss
  2) **Utmost good faith** – the parties to a contract of insurance are expected to be truthful
  3) **Indemnity** – the principle by which the policyholder shall be put in the same financial position after a loss as she or he was in before the loss took place
  4) **Proximate cause** – the principle of insurance states that the insurer is not only liable for loss caused directly by a risk insured against, but also for losses incurred indirectly, for example, fire

insurance would not only cover losses as a result of fire but also damage caused by the fire service fighting the fire.

Insurance Proposal Form   A form completed by a person seeking insurance cover. Unless accurately completed insurance may be withdrawn.

Insurance Proposer   A person seeking insurance cover.

Insurance Syndicates   Groups of insurance underwriters. These groups work together to enable them to accept larger shares of risks than a single individual could manage. In addition, syndicates can group together underwriters who specialise in different fields of insurance cover.

Insurance Underwriters   The only people allowed to accept insurance at Lloyd's. Underwriters are backed by their own personal wealth and they have unlimited liability to indemnify insurance claims made against them. (See also Insurance Syndicates)

Insured   The person who has taken out insurance cover.

Insured Sum   The value for which property is insured, and the maximum amount which the insurance company will pay in any claim. Insurance cover which is not sufficient to cover the maximum possible loss or damage is referred to as Under Insurance.

Intangible Assets   Items that cannot easily be measured in money terms but which are considered valuable. Some examples are, the goodwill of a business, patents, and trademarks.

INTELPOST   The Royal Mail facsimile transmission service in the UK.

Inter Bank Rate   The rate of interest for loans between banks or the Euromarket.

Interest   The 'price' of borrowing money or the 'reward' for lending money (for example, to a bank). It is usually charged or allowed at so much per cent per annum.

Interest Warrant   The orders for the payment of interest on Government stock which is due to the stockholder.

Interface   A device used to link up a microcomputer with other equipment such as a printer.

Interim Dividend   A dividend usually paid about half-way through a company's financial year pending the final dividend which is declared when the full trading figures are known.

Interim Report   A report of any date other than the end of the fiscal year, such as the half-yearly report of a company in which profits and losses for the six months are disclosed. It can also be a report of a non-financial type.

Intermediary   A person who acts as a mediator or agent between parties – a go-between.

Internal Auditing   An appraisal of internal operations of an enterprise, carried out by the organisation's staff employees.

Internal Economies of Scale   Economies of scale that arise due to the growth of a firm. (See External Economies of Scale)

International Monetary Fund (IMF)   A fund composed of the currencies of contributing (member) countries and administered by them. The objectives of the IMF are to assist nations with a temporary balance of payments problem, and to provide economic guidelines to countries with permanent foreign trading problems.

International Trade   Trade which involves movement of goods over national boundaries.

International Union of Credit and Investment Insurers (Berne Union)   An international organisation whose function is to exchange information on the credit worthiness of companies in different countries

Intestate   A person who has died without leaving a Will.

Intra Vires   Within the powers. A term used in business in the context of a company's object object clause or directors' duties.

Inventory   A detailed list of articles, goods, stock, property, etc., held by a business, or in a property leased.

Invested Capital   The amount of money that is contributed to an enterprise by its owners.

Investment   To put money into some form of enterprise (for example, property, shares, assets) with the expectation of profit in return.

Investment Banks   The US equivalent of the UK issuing houses.

Investment Trust   A company formed to buy shares of other companies using the money they get from the sale of shares in their own company.

Invisible Trade   A term used in relation to international or foreign trade to refer to the buying and selling of services such as insurance, shipping freights, tourism, etc.

Invoice   A document sent by the seller to the buyer listing the goods that the buyer should have received and detailing expected payment. The invoice may also show details of any discounts offered.

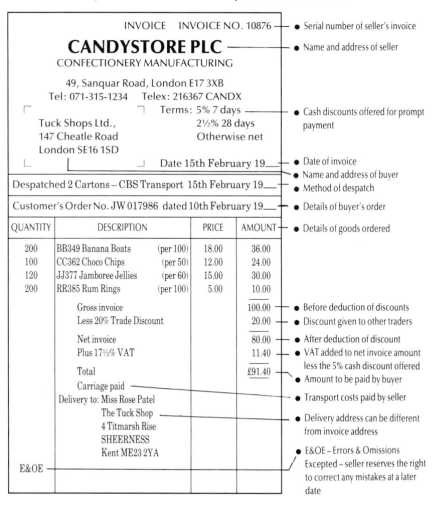

	INVOICE INVOICE NO. 10876			— ● Serial number of seller's invoice

CANDYSTORE PLC — ● Name and address of seller
CONFECTIONERY MANUFACTURING

49, Sanquar Road, London E17 3XB
Tel: 071-315-1234   Telex: 216367 CANDX

Terms: 5% 7 days ——— ● Cash discounts offered for prompt
Tuck Shops Ltd.,   2½% 28 days   payment
147 Cheatle Road   Otherwise net
London SE16 1SD

Date 15th February 19___ ● Date of invoice
● Name and address of buyer

Despatched 2 Cartons – CBS Transport 15th February 19___ ● Method of despatch

Customer's Order No. JW 017986 dated 10th February 19___ ● Details of buyer's order

QUANTITY	DESCRIPTION		PRICE	AMOUNT	● Details of goods ordered
200	BB349 Banana Boats	(per 100)	18.00	36.00	
100	CC362 Choco Chips	(per 50)	12.00	24.00	
120	JJ377 Jamboree Jellies	(per 60)	15.00	30.00	
200	RR385 Rum Rings	(per 100)	5.00	10.00	
	Gross invoice			100.00	● Before deduction of discounts
	Less 20% Trade Discount			20.00	● Discount given to other traders
	Net invoice			80.00	● After deduction of discount
	Plus 17½% VAT			11.40	● VAT added to net invoice amount
	Total			£91.40	less the 5% cash discount offered
					● Amount to be paid by buyer
	Carriage paid				● Transport costs paid by seller
	Delivery to: Miss Rose Patel				
	The Tuck Shop				● Delivery address can be different
	4 Titmarsh Rise				from invoice address
	SHEERNESS				
	Kent ME23 2YA				● E&OE – Errors & Omissions
E&OE					Excepted – seller reserves the right

Excepted – seller reserves the right
to correct any mistakes at a later
date

Invoice Discounting A facility where a company may sell its invoices for less than their true value in order to obtain immediate payment.

Irredeemable Stock A term used to describe a type of security sold on The Stock Exchange, where there is no date quoted for repayment of funds invested.

Irrevocable Documentary Credit A credit arrangement that cannot be reversed or altered without the consent of all parties.

Irrevocable Letter of Credit A letter of credit which cannot be cancelled by the issuing bank or the accountee without the consent of the beneficiary.

Issue To write or print and then distribute, for example, share issue.

Issued Capital The amount of shares issued by a company in exchange for cash.

Issue Price The price at which a security is first sold by the issuer.

Issuing House An organisation involved in assisting the raising of company finance by sponsoring the launch of shares or other securities on behalf of their clients, or acting as intermediaries between companies seeking capital and those willing to provide it. An issuing house arranges the details of an issue of stock or shares, and the necessary compliance with Stock Exchange regulations in connection with its listing.

Itinerant Traders Door to door sales people such as hawkers and pedlars.

Job The particular work that someone is employed to carry out.

Job Analysis A detailed study of a job, often used to help in the formation of a job description.

Job Costing An analysis of a proposed job or contract to enable an estimate to be made of expected cost of carrying it out.

Job Description A broad general statement of the work required of an employee in respect of a specific job. The statement will include:

- Job title
- Details of duties and responsibilities
- Place or department where work is to be carried out

- Special features or skills/qualifications related to the job
- Supervision and assessment arrangements.

Job description

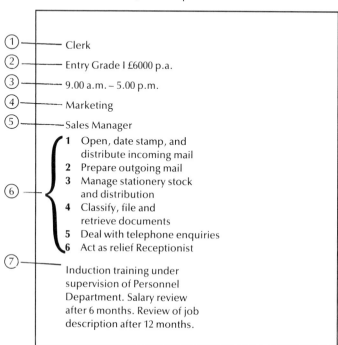

1. Job title
2. Grade/salary
3. Hours of employment
4. Department to work in
5. Responsible to
6. Functions, duties and responsibilities
7. Supervision and assessment procedures

Job Enlargement   Making the content of a job as big as possible and enlarging an original task to encompass several other activities.

Job Enrichment   The building into a job the scope for the worker's own way of doing things and for the worker to take responsibility for work with which they are involved, for example, their own ideas, ways of doing things, and self-assessment.

Job Evaluation   The assessment of the qualities required of people to carry out various jobs and the value of the activities involved to the organisation, for example, identifying induction training required and whether this would be cost-effective.

Job Order   A written statement authorising the production of a specific number of units of a product, performance of specific services, or construction or repair of equipment.

Job Satisfaction   The extent to which a person enjoys or values the work that they do. Although wages are an important factor in encouraging a person to work well there are many other reasons other than wages that make a job seem worthwhile doing, for example, working conditions, colleagues, appreciation by others, working hours, fringe benefits, etc.

Job Specification   A detailed statement drawn up from the job description and it contains references to the qualities required of a candidate for a specific job. This will include:

- Responsibilities involved
- Qualifications and past experience needed
- Skills of initiative or judgement necessary
- Physical fitness required
- Personal characteristics considered important.

Joint Account   An account, for example, bank account, in the names of two or more people. A mandate signed by all parties upon opening the account states how the account is to be operated, for example, any one person to sign cheques. In the absence of a mandate all parties are required to sign. Upon death of one of the parties the credit balance is vested in the survivors.

Joint Consultation   Discussions between employers and employees' representatives on matters of joint concern, for example, plans to improve safety or working conditions.

Joint Cost　The cost of facilities or services that are used in the output of two or more related activities, services, or products.

Joint Stock Company　A private or a public limited company which has many owners, called shareholders, each with a share in the company, and each with limited liability.

Joint Tenancy　Where property is owned by two or more persons. It is characteristic that on the death of one joint tenant that the survivor(s) take the property.

Judgement　A decision passed by a court as a result of legal proceedings and enforceable by law.

Justification　The process of arranging a line of text so that all lines end at the same point and there is a straight line down both the left and right sides/margins. This is achieved by adjusting the spaces between words or letters.

K (Kilobyte)　Unit of memory size used in computing. K = 1024 bytes. A byte is a set of bits (usually eight) which is used to represent one character.

Kangaroo Court　An irregular court.

Kerb Market　An unofficial market in stocks and shares, often carried on outside official trading hours.

Keyboard　The piece of hardware used to enter data into a computer.

Keystroke　A term sometimes used to refer to each strike of a key on a keyboard

Kite　A commercial term for a negotiable paper drawn without any actual transaction of assets and designed to obtain money on credit, and to give an impression of affluence. For example, depositing a cheque in a bank account to give a good impression, but knowing that a cheque issued elsewhere will cancel the value of the deposit. The time required to clear these cheques through the banking system makes it possible to steal in this manner. Behaving in this way is sometimes referred to as Kite Flying

Kitemark　A symbol, in the form of a kite, of quality and reliability allowed to be displayed on articles approved by the British Standards Institution as having reached standards laid down by them.

Knock for Knock   An agreement whereby each insurer pays for damage to its policyholder's car, regardless of who was to blame, providing the policy covers own damage.

Labour   The factor of production which is mankind's physical and mental contribution to the creation of goods and services. It is the factor which converts resources into goods and services which others want. This contribution to production is rewarded with wages, profits, or interest. All production requires some labour. Even the automated factory requires workers to supervise machinery, program computers to operate equipment and process paperwork, etc. Therefore, it is important that there should be an adequate supply of labour, containing the appropriate skills required, whether they be for unskilled, specialist, or professional workers.

Labourer   An unskilled manual worker.

Labour Intensive   The production processes requiring a high proportion of labour to machinery (capital).

Labour Turnover   An average measurement of how frequently a workforce is replaced over a period of time.

Laden Weight   The weight of a vehicle, including its load.

Laissez Faire   Unrestricted freedom in commerce.

Lame Duck   A person or business that is ineffectual.

Land   The factor of production that includes not only geographical area but all natural resources found in the earth and sea. Land in this sense includes:

- geographical surface area
- rivers, lakes and seas
- minerals and chemicals.

Landing Order   A Customs document issued after payment of duty and giving permission for goods to be unloaded from a ship.

Landlord   A person who owns and leases property to a tenant or who owns or runs a lodging house, inn, etc.

Land Waiter   An officer of the Customs Department who examines goods liable to duty.

Larceny A technical term for theft.

Laser Printer A computer printer giving very high quality print.

Laser Scanner Equipment that uses a laser to read bar codes on items and to transfer information to a computer.

Launder To convert money obtained illegally into a form whereby it is used legally.

Lay Days The number of days permitted for the loading or unloading of a ship without incurring demurrage (compensation).

Layperson A person who does not have specialised or professional knowledge of a subject.

Lay Off To dismiss from employment temporarily.

Lawyer A member of the legal profession, for example, solicitor, trained and qualified to advise and represent others in legal matters.

Law Suit A proceeding in a court of law brought by one party against another.

Lead A term sometimes used in business to refer to information that could result in a sale to a prospective customer.

Leadership Qualities held by a person that enable them to motivate others.

Leadership Styles The four basic styles of leadership:

1) **Autocratic** – where the leader takes decisions and expects others to carry out these decisions without question
2) **Persuasive** – where the leader takes the lead in taking decisions but spends time persuading others that these decisions are correct
3) **Consultative** – where the views of the group are taken into account before decisions are made, although the leader has the final say in the decision.
4) **Democratic** – where the leader allows a decision to emerge through group discussions.

Lead Time A term used in manufacturing to refer to the time between the design of a product and its production.

Leakage An allowance made for partial loss (stock, etc) due to leaking of liquids. The term is also sometimes used in business to refer to loss of merchandise through staff dishonesty (pilfering), thefts by the public (shoplifting) and stock deterioration.

Lease   A contract by which legal title to property is transferred to a person for a specified period, for example, lease of a factory building by the owner to a firm for ten years.

Lease Back   A property transaction in which the buyer leases property purchased back to the seller.

Leasehold   Land or property held under lease.

Lease Holder   A person in possession of leasehold property.

Legacy   A gift by will of money or personal property.

Legal Aid   Financial assistance authorised by law to assist people on very low incomes to obtain legal advice and representation in legal disputes.

Legal Tender   Any means of payment which must be accepted by law in settlement of a debt.

Lender of Last Resort   The term used for the situation when the commercial banks run short of cash and they recall deposits they have in the money market. This leaves the discount houses short of funds. The Bank of England 'lends as a last resort' to the discount houses, but at a higher rate of interest than that obtainable elsewhere in the money market. In most countries the Central Bank acts as 'lender of last resort'.

Lessee   The person who is leasing or renting property from another person.

Lessor   The person who is leasing or renting property from another person or company.

Letter of Allotment   A letter sent to applicants for shares in a public company telling them how many shares they have been allocated as a result of their application.

Letter of Administration/Attorney   A formal document giving a person legal authority to act on behalf of another.

Letter of Credit   An undertaking by a bank to honour bills of exchange drawn against it up to a specified amount provided certain conditions are met, for example, goods are supplied by a specified date.

Letter of Credit at Sight   A letter of credit in which a bank promises to pay in cash immediately once its conditions are met. This is also known as D/P terms.

Letter for Credit Acceptance   A letter of credit in which a bank promises to accept bills of exchange requiring payment at some future date providing its conditions are met. This is also known as D/A terms.

Letter of Hypothecation   A letter from an exporter to their bank. It authorises the bank to sell goods being exported, for the best price they can get, if the bank cannot obtain payment on a bill of exchange drawn on the importer. The exporter agrees to make good any loss incurred.

Liabilities   The legal obligations or debts owed by an individual or an organisation to others, or obligations which are likely to arise in the future.

Licence   An official document giving permission to someone to do something that would be illegal without the licence, for example, drive a car, export explosives, etc.

Licence, Credit   The licence issued by the Director General of Fair Trading in the UK to all lenders (under regulated agreements) credit brokers (those who introduce people to sources of credit), debt collectors, credit agencies, etc. The Director General ensures that the licensee is a fit person to hold a licence.

Licence, Export   Goods (for example, explosives, works of art, etc.) cannot be taken out of the country without permission. This permission is signified by provision of an export licence issued by Customs officials.

Licensed Deposit Taker (LDT)   Every financial institution that accepts deposits in order to re-lend (for example, banks) requires a licence from The Bank of England to operate. Licence holders are categorised as a 'Recognised Bank' or a 'Licensed Deposit Taker (LDT)'.

Life Assurance   (See Insurance)

LIFO   The abbreviation for last in, first out. A stock control term implying that the most recently received items are sold first, leaving the oldest items on the shelf. (See also FIFO.)

Limited Company   A company owned by two or more shareholders whose liability is limited to the value of the shares held. A limited company is said to have a corporate identity, that is, an identity separate from that of the owners. It can sue and be sued in its title name.

Limited Liability   The liability of the shareholders for the debts of a business which is limited to the amount they have invested in the business and not their personal assets.

Limited Partnership   A partnership with partners who have limited liability (i.e. limited partners). However, there must be at least one general partner who has unlimited liability.

Line Management   A management term referring to the line of responsibility from the head of an organisation through the various levels of personnel to the managers actually providing the product or service the company provides.

Liner   A ship whose primary trade is providing passenger transport, usually deep sea.

Liquidation   The process of terminating (winding up) the affairs of a business by selling off its assets in order to discharge its liabilities. Liquidation may be caused by bankruptcy or by choice of the owners.

Liquidator   A person assigned to supervise the liquidation of a business. The legal authorisation, rights, and duties of such a person vary according to whether the liquidation is compulsory or voluntary.

Liquid Capital Ratio   The ratio of quick current assets to current liabilities. Quick assets are cash and items readily convertible into cash but not stocks or work in progress. It is a measure of a firm's ability to meet its short-term liabilities and is sometimes called the 'acid test ratio'. It is calculated as follows:

$$\frac{\text{current assets minus stocks and work in progress}}{\text{current liabilities}}$$

Liquidity   The ease with which the assets of a business can be turned into cash is known as liquidity.

Liquidity Ratio   The ratio of liquid assets to eligible liabilities. This ratio is an important factor in determining the amount of money a bank is willing to lend to a business.

Listed Company (Quoted Company)   A company whose shares are listed and quoted on The Stock Exchange.

Listing Agreement   The Listing Agreement is a set of rules to which all companies whose shares are listed on The Stock Exchange must abide. Any breach of the rules of the Listing Agreement can result in suspension of dealing in the company's shares.

List Price The selling price of merchandise as quoted in a catalogue, price list, or advertisement.

Lloyd's Register of Shipping A publication which classifies ships according to their type of construction and condition. This originated from the need of marine insurers for accurate information about ships. Every vessel over 100 tons is on the register, but only those that conform to certain standards are classified. The following are the classification standards that are used:

- A Maltese Cross indicates it was built under surveillance of Lloyd's engineers
- The letter indicates the condition of the hull
- The number indicates the condition of the ship's equipment.

Loan A sum of money lent for a period of time in return for repayment of the principal sum and a charge for interest.

Loan Account A facility offered by banks. A sum of money is advanced to a customer's current account for a set period of time. The loan is repaid by regular, fixed sums, until the loan and the interest charged is paid off.

Loan Co-operative A co-operative which arranges loans or mortgages for its members at rates cheaper than those which could be obtained on the open market. Members can borrow or deposit money with these co-operatives.

Loan Stock (See Debentures)

Local Authority Undertakings This refers to enterprises run by local authorities employing direct labour, for example, bus services, banqueting suites, sports centres.

Location of Industry (See Industry, Location of)

Loco Price The overseas ex-warehouse price, sometimes quoted in foreign currency. All charges must be paid by the importer from the place the goods lie, i.e., all transit, insurance, dock and on and off-loading charges.

London Air Freight Market   A market, formed in 1946 in the Baltic Exchange, which enables brokers representing airline companies to meet brokers representing clients. The majority of UK air charters (including package tours) are arranged through this market.

London Commodity Market (Exchange)   A group of exchanges providing a 'futures' market in tea, coffee, cocoa, spices, sugar, dried fruit, vegetable oil, soya bean, rubber, and others.

Long-Term Liability   A liability which a firm does not have to pay in the short-term.

Loss   The amount by which the costs of a business transaction or operation exceed its revenue.

Loss Leader   A term used to refer to a commonly-bought product being sold at no profit or even at below cost price in the hope that customers attracted by it will buy other products, and thereby compensate for any losses made.

Loss Ratio   The ratio of annual losses sustained to the premiums received by an insurance company.

Lot   An item or set of items for sale in an auction.

Low Geared   A term which refers to a company whose capital is mainly financed by ordinary shares.

Luncheon Vouchers   Slips of paper which can be exchanged as part payment against the cost of meals or food in shops and restaurants participating in the scheme. The vouchers are issued, in various denominations, by employers to workers.

Lutine Bell   The name of a bell taken from the sunken ship *Lutine*. The bell is kept at Lloyd's in London and is rung before important announcements, especially a major loss. One chime is used to indicate bad news and two chimes for good news.

Luxembourg   The capital city of the Grand-Duchy of Luxembourg and it is also the home of the European Court of Justice, the Court of Auditors, the Secretariat and the Statistical Service of the European Parliament.

Mail Order　The purchase of goods or services by post rather than through a shop.

There are a variety of types of mail order business:

• Through part-time agents
• Direct catalogue selling
• Direct advertising (press and magazines).

Mail Shot　A standard advertisement sent to many prospective customers by post.

Mainframe Computer　A large computer which has many terminals.

Managed Bonds　A type of bond introduced by the unit trust groups and life offices where the underlying assets may be changed at the discretion of the management.

Management　The senior members of an enterprise who decide and direct the policies and aims of the operation.

Management by Objectives (MBO)　A system of management whereby performance of personnel is assessed against mutually agreed objectives. The system involves a broad statement of the company aims to be achieved over a given period. This is focused into objectives for departments or individuals, and assessment of the extent to which the objectives are achieved.

Managing Director　A company director appointed by the Board of Directors to run the organisation on a day-to-day basis and to carry out policies of the Board.

Mandate　A document giving one party the legal authority to act on behalf of another. For example, a standing order mandate raised by one of its customers can give a bank the authority to make payments out of their account to someone else.

Manifest　A summary of all the bills of lading and cargo a ship is carrying.

Manufacturing Expense　The production costs other than those for direct labour and raw materials.

Margin　The profit on a transaction.

Marginal　A term used by economists to denote a change in the total of one variable resulting from a small change in another.

Marginal Cost   The increase or decrease in total cost that materialises if the output is increased or decreased by one unit.

Marginal Product   The change in total quantity produced as a result of a change in the quantity used of one or more resources of production.

Marginal Revenue   The increase in total revenue that is achieved by selling one additional unit.

Marginal Utility   Utility refers to the satisfaction which is obtained from a product or service. The term marginal utility can be defined as the satisfaction received from possessing one extra unit of a commodity or the satisfaction lost by giving up one unit.

Marine Insurance   The class of insurance specialising in providing cover for ships and their cargoes. The main world market is at Lloyds of London.

Mark Down   The reduction of an originally higher price, for example, reduction of a retail price.

Market   Any organisation that enables buyers and sellers to make contact to arrange deals, for example, stock exchange, foreign exchange markets, commodity markets, street market, world market.

Market Appraisal   A systematic investigation of factors influencing demand for goods or services.

Market Capitilisation   This is calculated by multiplying the market price of a company's shares by the total number of shares issued. It indicates a company's market value.

Market Coverage   The extent to which sales or advertising has reached the target audience.

Marketing   The process of selling products or services. It begins with an examination of what people want from a product or service (market research). This is followed by an assessment of how to produce the product or service (product development) that will satisfy that requirement, and at the same time make a profit in the process. The next stage is to develop a marketing strategy that will get the product to the appropriate market at a competitive price. This will involve creating an advertising campaign that is backed by selling and distribution procedures.

Marketing Mix All the considerations that a firm makes in marketing its goods or services. Includes price, place, product and promotion.

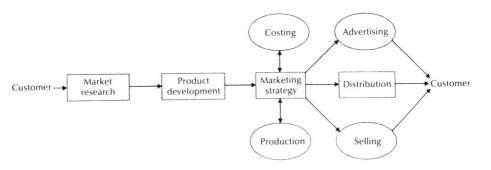

Flow chart to show how the marketing process in developed

Marketing Board An organisation set up by the UK government for certain agricultural products to regulate production, distribution and prices.

Market Maker A Stock Exchange Member Firm which is prepared to buy or sell shares at all times, thus 'making a market' in them. Market Makers can operate on the Stock Exchange floor, off-floor, or both on- and off-floor. They 'make a market' in shares by being prepared to buy or sell shares at all times to and from Broker/Dealers. They may deal direct with the Broker/Dealers on the Exchange floor, or indirect through the Stock Exchange Automated Quotation System (SEAQ), whereas Broker/Dealers are not permitted to operate in this way. (See also Broker/Dealers and SEAQ)

Market Order An instruction to a broker to sell or buy at the best price currently available on the market.

Market Overt A public market where goods are openly displayed for sale. In a market overt stolen goods remain the property of the buyer unless the original thief is prosecuted and convicted.

Market Price The prevailing price, as determined by supply and demand, at which goods, services, etc., may be bought or sold.

Market Research   The collection and analysis of data relating to the demand for a product, often undertaken before marketing it. It could be said to be research into 'Who wants what, why and when?'

Market Town   A town that holds a regular market, for example, street market or agricultural centre.

Market Value   The value of an asset determined by the actual amount for which similar assets are currently being purchased.

Mark-Up   This refers to the percentage profit which is added to the cost price by a trader to establish the selling price. For example, if an article has a cost price of 80p and it is to be sold for £1, the mark-up is:

$$\frac{\text{(amount added)}}{\text{(cost price)}} \quad \frac{20}{80} \times 100 = 25\%$$

(See also Profit Margin)

Marine Insurance   Insurance covering risks at sea, including cover of ships and their cargo.

Mass Production   Production on a large scale to a standardised pattern by means of extensive mechanisation and division of labour.

Matrix Management   A form of management based on project teams drawn from two or more departments of the organisation.

Maturity   The date when an obligation becomes due, for example, the date on which a bill or similar document falls due and is legally payable.

Media   The collective term used to refer to the means of mass communications, including television, radio, newspapers and magazines.

Media Evaluation   A consideration of the alternative media for advertising available before a final choice is made.

Meeting   An assembly or gathering of people – shareholders, management, workers, etc. Meetings are an important method of direct communication within an organisation. They give the opportunity for exchange of ideas and collective efforts to solve problems and to formulate policies. They also provide a convenient means of issuing instructions or information to many people at one time. The principal officers of a meeting are the Chairperson, Secretary and Treasurer:

- The Chairperson is responsible for the conduct of the meeting
- The Secretary sends out notices of the meeting and a copy of the agenda, records minutes and ensures meeting decisions are carried out

- The Treasurer is responsible for financial matters. Sometimes the jobs of secretary and treasurer are combined.

There are three basic types of meeting:

1) **General** – open to all members of the organisation. These are held monthly, quarterly or annually (annual general meeting – AGM), and are used for committee members to communicate with all members of the organisation. The AGM also serves as a useful time for re-election of principal officers

2) **Extra-ordinary** – additional general meeting called to discuss some special or unexpected event

3) **Committee** – only attended by committee members, these deal with a specific aspect of the organisation's function. Committees report back to a full general meeting.

Meeting of Creditors   A meeting of the creditors of a business which must take place within fourteen days after a receiving order has been made.In the case of a company in liquidation the meeting is called to appoint a liquidator or to determine the wishes of the creditors.

Member   A person belonging to an organisation.

Member Firm   A firm of Broker/Dealers which is a corporate Member of The Stock Exchange.

Member States   The 12 member countries of the EC. These are Belgium, Denmark, France, Germany, Greece, Ireland, Italy, Luxembourg, The Netherlands, Portugal, Spain and the United Kingdom. The total population is approximately 322 million. A recent agreement with EFTA will result in a 19-nation economic bloc from 1993. (See also European Free Trade Association.)

MEP   Member of the European Parliament.

Memorandum   A form of printed communication used within an organisation.

Anderson, Page & Tate	Solicitors	MEMORANDUM

FROM: G Anderson   TO: L Tate
DATE: 20 October 1991   SUBJECT: Mrs B Booth   REF: GA/LT

I have received a letter from Mr P White claiming damages on behalf of his client, Mrs B Booth. Please investigate this by getting Mr Brayson's side of the affair and report back to me in three days.

Memorandum of Association   One of the documents which is sent to the Registrar of Companies when a new company is formed. The document states the external relationship of a company, that is, the relationship between the firm and others. It defines the constitution and powers of a company and the scope of its activities. It is the document which ensures that the stated aims of the company are legal and proper.

Memory   The storage of information on a computer. Expressed in Kilobytes or Megabytes.

Menu   The list of processing options displayed on a computer screen from which choices can be made.

Merchant   A person who trades on their own account for profit.

Merchantable Quality   Goods sold must be of merchantable quality. This means that goods must be reasonably fit for their normal purpose, bearing in mind the price paid, the nature of the goods and how they were described. Thus a new item must not be damaged and must work properly.

Merchant Banks   Institutions which have built up a reputation of giving advice and dealing in such things as foreign exchange, raising of capital, mergers and takeovers and a whole range of services particularly for larger businesses. (See Issuing House and Offer for Sale)

Merchant Wholesaler   A wholesale trader who buys goods and later sells them to make a profit. He is independent and does not act on the behalf of anyone. (See Wholesaler)

Merger   When two or more firms combine to operate under a single control. The most familiar way in which a merger takes place is for one company to absorb the other by a 'take-over' bid. A bid is made to take over control of another company by offering money, or money and so many shares of the bidding company, in exchange for shares of the firm being taken over. To make the task of taking over a firm easier, the firm seeking control of another may buy up the voting shares on the open market until it owns sufficient to make a strong take-over bid. Once the take-over has been effected the firm may be in a stronger trading position and enjoy greater economies of scale.

MICR   Magnetic ink character recognition. Characters can be 'read' by a computer's optical reader. Banks use this system to process cheques through their computer. Just above the bottom of a cheque are characters showing the cheque number, bank and branch and customers account number. The amount of the cheque is encoded when the cheque enters the clearing system. This allows the cheque to be processed automatically.

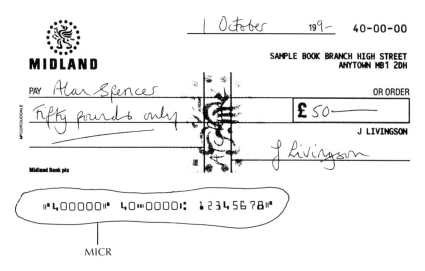

MICR

A computer can read certain numbers which are written in magnetic ink. You can see these numbers printed on the bottom of the cheque.

Microcomputer   A general term used to describe a small personal computer such as a desktop or laptop model.

Microfiche   A single sheet of microfilm containing a large number of 'pictures' of documents. These can be viewed by using a 'reader' or 'scanner' which magnifies the images and displays it on a viewer or VDU. The process saves document storage space.

Middleman   An intermediary. An independent trader engaged in the distribution of goods from the producer to the consumer.

Migrant Worker   A citizen of one country who lives and works in another.

Mini Computer   A computer that is smaller than a mainframe computer (very large) but larger than a microcomputer (very small). A mini computer may have several terminals.

Minimum Balance   The minimum credit balance required by a bank to conduct a personal customer's account free of charges.

Minimum Lending Rate (MLR)   The officially announced lowest rate in the UK at which the Bank of England will lend money to the discount market. All other interest rates tend to follow MLR movement when used in this way. The use of MLR is currently suspended, although it can be activated at some future date, possibly temporarily.

Minor   Anybody who is under the age of eighteen in the UK.

Minutes   The written or typed summary record of what has taken place at a meeting. They sometimes include a verbatim report, which is a word for word record of a statement. The minutes are recorded by the secretary and have to be communicated to those present for acceptance.

Minutes of Meeting

A meeting of the Safety Committee of Daly Designs Ltd. held in the Conference Room on Monday 14th July 19— at 1700 hrs.

Present

Mr. P. Mahoney (Chairman)
Miss J. Shaw
Mrs. J. Jones

Mr. T. Cryer (Security)
Miss E. Ginger (Secretary)

1   Apologies for Absence
The Secretary reported that Mr. Flowers was unable to attend due to illness.

2   Minutes of the Last Meeting
The Minutes of the last meeting had been circulated previously, were approved, and signed by the Chairman.

3   Matters arising from the Minutes
There were no matters arising.

4   Correspondence
The Secretary read a letter from Five Star Insurance who advised that the Company's buildings insurance cover be increased by 8%. It was agreed that this recommendation should be put into immediate effect.

5   Secretary's Report
This had been circulated prior to the meeting and was accepted.

6   Security Officer's Report
The Security Officer reported that the recent fire drill was very successful and appeared to have been taken seriously by employees.

7   Safety Notices
Concern was expressed that many safety notices were now old and damaged and it was agreed that the Secretary would purchase replacements urgently.

8   Any Other Business
There was no other business.

9   Date and Time of Next Meeting
This was fixed for Monday 16th October, 19— at 1700 hrs. in the Conference Room.

P. MAHONEY
Chairman
21st July 19—

Misrepresentation To falsely represent; to give a misleading interpretation.

Mixed Economy An economy which consists of both State-owned and privately-owned enterprises.

MLR (See Minimum Lending Rate)

MMC Monopolies and Mergers Commission. A body that investigates and reports, on behalf of the Government, on mergers and monopolies in the UK.

Mobile Shop A shop contained within some form of vehicle and used to take goods for sale to customers doors.

Mobility An economic term which refers to the ease with which industry, labour and capital can transfer from one area to another.

- **Geographical mobility** – describes movement from one location to another
- **Occupational mobility** – describes movement between one job and another.

Modems Devices that allow computers to 'talk' over the telephone. There are two basic types.

1) Acoustic couplers that fit over the phone
2) Integral modems which are inside the machine.

Monetarism A name given to an economic doctrine which sees the money supply as central to the management of the economy.

Monetary Dealings in money matters.

Monetary Directives Instructions from the Bank of England to the banks to restrict the growth of borrowing and lending.

Monetary Policy The government policy with regard to the money supply and interest rates.

Money Anything that is acceptable as exchange.

Money at Call Loaned money which can be recalled immediately.

Money Broker Some firms who borrow from bankers and lend to others, aiming to profit by using different rates of interest.

Money, Functions of   Money has three basic functions.

1) A medium of exchange
2) A measure of value
3) A store of value.

Moneylender   A person who is registered under the Moneylenders Acts to lend money.

Money Market   A market consisting of the Bank of England, commercial banks, accepting and discount houses who lend or borrow between themselves.

Money, Qualities of   For something to be considered as money, or in the place of money, it must be:

• Durable (hard wearing)
• Divisable (easily divided into smaller units)
• Portable (convenient to carry)
• Acceptable (people must agree to its use).

Money Shops   A relatively recently introduced style of banking started by finance companies. They aim to provide a range of personal customer services such as mortgage facilities, insurance, investment advice, etc.

Money Supply   The government calculates several different measures of the money supply which include the following:

• **M0 (monetary base)** – consists mainly of notes and coins
• **M1 (narrow money)** – includes M0 plus any bank deposit which can be withdrawn without notice. About 80 per cent of M1 does not earn interest
• **M2 (transaction balances)** – is M1 plus any other deposits that can used for drawing cheques, and small deposits in bank deposit accounts
• **M3 (broad money)** – is M1 plus money in bank deposits which require notice before withdrawal.
• **PSL2 (private sector liquidity)** – is M3 plus money in building societies, National Savings Bank and other similar accounts.

Monitor   A special type of television which produces a clearer, defined picture when used with a computer. It is also sometimes referred to as the visual display unit or VDU.

Monopolies and Mergers Commission   The government watchdog which investigates monopolies.

Monopoly A situation where one person or organisation has complete control of a market for which there is no alternative substitute.

Monopsony A situation in which the whole market for a product or service consists of only one buyer.

Moonlighting The undertaking of work outside normal working hours, sometimes with the aim of avoiding payment of Income Tax.

Mortgage A long-term loan for the purchase of property, secured by the Deeds or Documents of Ownership.

Mortgage Debenture Loan stock which is secured against specific assets. If the loan is not repaid the debenture holders are entitled to the proceeds from the sale of the secured property.

Mortgagee The person to whom property is mortgaged.

Mortgagor A person who grants a mortgage.

MRP (See Resale Prices Act)

Multinational Company A company which has direct control over an organisation sited in more than one country.

Multiple Stores Large retail organisations with stores in many towns. The link between them is the common name of ownership. They are also referred to as chain stores.

Municipal Undertakings Enterprises carried out by local government, for example, swimming pools, banqueting rooms, libraries, etc.

Mutilated Notes Bank notes that are soiled or damaged or have parts missing. Banks will exchange these but application for payment must be made to the Bank of England.

My Word is My Bond The motto of The Stock Exchange.

National Consumers' Council An organisation set up by the UK government in 1975 to carry out research into consumer problems and to present consumers' views to the government, the Director General of Fair Trading, and to industry. It acts as a pressure group and has strong links with other consumer organisations.

National Debt The total amount owed for loans raised by successive governments, on which fixed interest is paid.

National Economic Development Council (NEDC)   An advisory body on general economic policy in the UK, composed of representatives of government, management, and trade unions.

National Giro   A banking system run in the UK by National Girobank through post offices. All accounts are held centrally and a comprehensive range of services are offered.

National Insurance   The name of the UK State welfare scheme (for example, health services). Payments towards the scheme are deducted from each payment of wages.

Nationalisation   The take-over of a private firm by the Government. Previously led to the formation of British Rail, British Coal and others.

National Savings   A State operated savings system in the UK offering a variety of schemes aimed mainly at the small saver.

National Savings Certificates   A government bond in the UK. The State is responsible for repayment of capital and interest.

Naturalisation   The process whereby citizenship of a country is given to someone of foreign birth.

Natural Monopoly   An area of business which is considered most effective when there is a single, large monopolistic supplier, for example, gas and water.

Natural Resources   The primary products obtained from the earth. These include gas, water, fish, ore and minerals, etc.

Near Money   Assets which can relatively easily be turned into cash and, therefore, are considered to be 'near to money'.

Negligence   A breach of legal duty to take reasonable care and precaution in one's duties. Such failure makes a person liable for any damages or losses suffered.

Negotiable Instrument   A document that entitles the holder to a certain sum of money. Such a document is said to be negotiable if its ownership is transferable to another person. In the case of a bank note or a bearer cheque ownership passes to another person simply by handing over the document. On the other hand, an order cheque or a bill of exchange requires endorsement (a signature) before they can be passed to another person.

Negotiable Irrevocable Letter of Credit A letter of credit whose irrevocable commitments extend to whoever is the bearer.

Negotiation A financial term referring to the act of transferring the property of a bill from one person to another. The term is also used to refer to the discussions that take place to try an achieve a settlement or agreement, for example, in an industrial dispute.

Net The amount reached after all deductions have been taken. For example, net wage is the figure reached after deductions have been taken away from gross wage.

Net Capital Formation The total amount of capital assets which a country has created over a given period, less any depreciation during the same period.

Net Cash The trading terms when no discount is offered on the quoted price of goods and payment is expected in a relatively short time.

Net Income Revenue less operating costs.

Net Investment The amount of investment after making allowance for depreciation of capital.

Net Loss The excess of the sum of expenses and losses over that of revenues and income.

Net Proceeds The profits from the sale of property less the costs that are directly associated with the property.

Net Profit The profit after all expenses have been deducted. One way this can be calculated is gross profit less running costs.

Net Profit on Sales The balance remaining after deductions from gross profit of selling expenses and other expenses that vary directly with sales.

Net Purchases The cost of all purchases less less returns and allowances and any discounts given.

Net Weight The weight of a product excluding its packaging.

Network A computer system containing several linked terminals.

Net Worth The value of a firm to its owners, calculated by the total assets minus liabilities owed to outsiders.

New Issues Market The market for new shares, i.e. shares which are not yet sold on The Stock Exchange.

Next of Kin The next in line or nearest blood relative.

NIC Newly industrialised countries.

Night Safe A facility provided by banks at many branches to enable customers to make deposits after the bank is closed. A box or wallet is provided by the bank for the deposits which are placed in a special safe which has an opening in the outside wall of the bank.

No Claims Bonus A discount on the premium payable if the insurance is to be renewed and no claim for indemnity has been filed in the previous insurance period. The system is particularly applied to motor insurance.

Nominal Capital The amount of capital of a company authorised by its Memorandum of Association.

Nominal Partner Someone who is not a partner but takes an active part in the management of a partnership.

Nominal Payment A small amount paid as a token to signify that some payment has been made.

Nominal Price The nearest market price of goods or securities in which there is little trade.

Nominal Price The face value stated for a security but which bears no relationship to the market value.

Nominee A person who is named in a transaction instead of the real person concerned.

Noncontrollable Costs The costs not subject to regulation at any level of managerial authority.

Noncumulative Dividend A return on preferred stock which, if passed, does not have to be made up at a later date.

Non-Insurable Risks Risks which insurance companies are unwilling to insure against. They may be too big or too small or not due to outside events, or their probability of occurrence may be incapable of estimation due to lack of statistics.

Non Profit Corporation An organisation, such as a charity or an educational institution, in which the stockholders do not share in the profits and losses.

Notice   The agreed period of time that an employee or an employer must give in order to terminate employment.

Not Negotiable   Something which cannot be sold or transferred to another person. However, a cheque can be transferred, but the new holder has no better right to the cheque than the previous owner. In other words, if someone accepted a stolen cheque as payment for a debt, the true owner of the cheque is entitled to the value of it.

Not Transferrable   A crossing placed on a cheque restricting its transferability. In effect it means that the cheque must be placed to the account of the named payee.

Nutritional Labelling   The nutritional information (for example fat present in food) given on packaging. The EC are in the process of establishing a standard format that will help to prevent confusion and misleading claims.

Objects Clause   A clause in the Memorandum of Association of a company which establishes what the purposes of the company are and how it might achieve its objectives. Two important aspects of the objects clause are the terms 'intravires' and 'ultra vires':

• **Intravires** – within the powers (of the organisation)
• **Ultravires** – beyond the powers (of the organisation).

(See Memorandum of Association)

Obsolesence   An asset which has lost in usefulness due to changes in style, technique, legislation, or other causes which have no physical relation to the asset itself.

Occupancy Expense   Rent, light, heat, depreciation and other expenses that relate to the use of property.

Occupations, Classification of   All occupations can be related to one of three categories – primary, secondary or tertiary. See the illustration on page 140.

Occupiers Liability Act 1957   An Act of the UK Parliament under which the occupier of property owes a 'common duty of care' to all visitors, to ensure that they will be reasonably safe when using the premises for a permitted purpose. However, warnings can free the owner from liability – for example, a notice saying: 'Beware! Men working overhead'. But the warning has to be adequate for visitors to

Classifications of occupations

be able to take precautions, and visitors themselves have a duty to take care. The occupier has no obligation to safeguard a trespasser's interests.

OECD (See Organisation for Economic Co-operation and Development)

Offer for Sale The method by which a company wishing to raise capital will sell new securities to a merchant bank acting as an Issuing House. The merchant bank then 'offers the shares for sale' to the public. Merchant banks play a major role in assisting in raising company finance by sponsoring first issues of company shares on behalf of their clients, or acting as intermediaries between companies seeking capital and those willing to provide it. (See also Merchant Banks)

Office of Fair Trading (OFT) The OFT is a UK government agency which:

- Publishes consumer advice information
- Encourages industries to form associations and Codes of Practice
- Investigates and prosecutes traders who persistently commit offences
- Checks on the fitness of traders who provide credit or hire agreements
- Make suggestions for changes in consumer law.

Official Receiver The Official Receiver in Bankruptcy is responsible for collecting the assets of a bankrupt, and disposing of them, and distributing the proceeds fairly between creditors.

Offset An accounting term which refers to a counterbalancing amount used to equalise some figure on the opposite side of the account.

OFTEL Office of Telecommunications. A statutory body with the function to represent the interests of consumers with regard to the UK telecommunications industry.

Oil Tankers Ships specially constructed to carry oil and oil products in bulk.

Oligopoly A market situation in which control over the supply of a commodity is held by a small number of producers each of whom is able to influence prices and thus affect the position of its competitors.

Ombudsmen An official (Commissioner) in the UK who investigates citizens' complaints against the Government or its servants. The Commissioners respond to complaints about a particular service, insist on examining relevant documents, and provide unbiased findings.

OPEC Organisation of Petroleum Producing Countries.

Open Account Any account which has not been finalised. For example, a loan that has not been repaid.

Open Cheque An uncrossed cheque which can be exchanged for cash at the bank on which it is drawn.

Open Indent Order An order which does not specify from which supplier or producer the goods should be obtained.

Opening Balance The contents of an account at the beginning of a period, as at the start of a new month or year.

Open Market Operations A method of monetary control whereby the central bank purchases and sells government securities on the open market, thus influencing the amount of money in circulation.

Operating Budget The budget which deals with operating income and expense, as opposed to capital expense.

Operating Expense An expense which occurs in the ordinary course of business of an enterprise. Marketing and administrative expenses fall into this category.

Operating Income   The figure which represents the direct revenues of a business after expenses have been deducted and excluding income realised from other sources.

Option   The right to buy or sell within a stated period, specified amounts of a particular stock or share at a pre-arranged price (called the 'striking price').

- **Put option** – the right to sell
- **Call option** – the right to buy.

Opportunity Cost   The true cost of something is the lost opportunity of making an alternative choice. For example, the opportunity cost of going to the cinema could be the alternative possibility of visiting a museum.

ORACLE   (See CEEFAX and TELETEXT)

Orderly Marketing Department   Price-fixing, anti-competitive agreements made between suppliers to limit the supply of goods to a market in order to keep prices artificially high

Ordinary Preference Share   (See Preference Share)

Ordinary Share   (See Shares)

Organisation and Method (O & M)   O & M originated in the British Civil Service during the 1940s, and is practised particularly in administrative departments. O & M is in fact the application of work study ideas to the office. It uses systematic analysis, with the objective of simplifying and improving office methods.

Organisation for Economic Co-operation and Development (OECD)   A group of rich countries, including Japan, America, Canada, Australia, New Zealand and West European nations, which aims to sustain economic growth and development and promote world trade. Its secretariat is based in Paris.

Origin Marking   The marking of goods with their place of origin. Following a European Court Case, Member States of the EC can no longer insist that goods imported from other Member States carry a 'made in' label, although manufacturers may label a product in this manner should they wish to do so.

Ostensible Partner   (See Nominal Partner)

Over-Capitilisation   (See Over-Trading)

Overdraft   One of the most common sources of business finance and is used for current rather than long-term needs. The bank customer is given permission to write out cheques for more money than they have in their account. The amount borrowed varies according to need. Since interest is only paid on the amount overdrawn on the account, the cost of borrowing varies as needs change. The overdraft is the limit to which the bank agrees an account may be overdrawn. However, the full limit may not be reached and the bank will only charge interest on the sums drawn which exceed the amount in the deposit.

Overheads   The general expenses of running a business such as rent, wages, heating, lighting, etc. These expenses do not vary closely with changes in output. They are sometimes referred to as fixed costs.

Over-Insurance   The buying of insurance to cover a value higher than the actual value of the item insured, although insurance will not compensate for other than the true value.

Overtime Ban   A ban on working overtime. Overtime provides a convenient way for employers to obtain extra working hours without taking on additional employees. When an overtime ban is in force the workers refuse to work additional hours.

Over-Trading   A situation where a firm has invested too much of its capital into fixed assets leaving it short of current assets, particularly cash.

Packaging   The outer wrapping of goods. As the packaging is a part of the cost of goods it is important to exploit this to the full by making it eyecatching and informative.

Pager   A lightweight receiver carried by a person which 'bleeps' when a signal is sent out to tell the holder to telephone some central point.

Pallet   A platform or tray which makes the lifting, stacking and transport of goods easier.

Paper Currency   Bank notes or documents which are legal tender and widely accepted as a means of payment.

Par or Par Value   Either the face or nominal value of a security, or the exact price that has been paid for it. A price higher than this is said to be 'above par', and lower 'below par'.

Parallel Imports   Goods bought in one EC Member State and resold in another. Importers may do this where the same product costs significantly more on the home market, to maximise profits. The practice promotes competition to the benefit of consumers, and is encouraged by the Commission.

Parent Company   A company which has a controlling interest in one or more subsidiary companies and which also operates on its own account. If a parent company has no trade or business of its own it is referred to as a 'holding company'.

Partnership   A business owned and run by two to twenty members, known as partners. They are commonly found in professions such as doctors, accountants, and solicitors. A deed of partnership sets out the rights of each partner, such as the way in which profits are to be divided. Where no deeds exist it is assumed that the profits are shared equally. All partners are equally responsible for the debts of the business. A 'sleeping' partner is one who invests in the business but takes no active part in running it, but such a partner is fully liable with other partners for debts incurred by the business. It is possible to have a limited partnership but at least one partner must accept unlimited liability. Consequently, limited partnerships are relatively rare.

Party Selling   A form of retailing where people, encouraged by the offer of commission, invite friends to a party, often in their own home, where goods (for example, cosmetics, lingerie, etc.) are offered for sale. Orders are taken by the host in exchange for a commission payment or gifts provided by the supplier.

Password   A word that needs to be typed into a computer to gain access to data it contains on restricted access.

Patent   The sole right granted (in letters of patent) to an inventor giving them the monopoly to make, use, and sell their invention for a limited period, and thus protecting against piracy.

Pawnbroker   A person who loans money with some article pledged as security by the borrower.

Pay Advice   A notice given to a worker telling them how their wage payment has been calculated. See the illustration on the opposite page.

Pay as You Earn (PAYE)   The system of paying Income Tax for most people in the UK. A contribution to the annual tax liability is taken from the individual by the employer and sent to the Tax Office.

Pay Advice		
FUTURE TECH. LIMITED ————————————		Employer
167 ———————————		Works number (identification number allotted to each employee)
1 APR 93		
N RUDGE		Employee
Tax Code	137L ————————	Indicates level of tax free allowances
Contribution letter	B	
N.I. No.	YK868347A ————	National Insurance number
Pay and allowances		
Basic Pay	420.94	
Total	420.94 ————————	Earnings before deductions (A)
Deductions (R = Refund)		
Income Tax	83.40 ————————	Tax on this instalment of wages
Nat. Insurance	11.58 ————————	Contributions to state welfare scheme
PENSION	27.89	
UNION	3.20 ————————	Voluntary deductions
Total	126.07 ————————	Total deductions (B)
Balances and totals to date		
Income Tax	166.80 ————————	Total income tax paid in the current year on the PAYE system
National Insurance	23.16 ————————	Total National Insurance contributions paid in the current year
Taxable Gross	786.10	Total gross wages earned to date
Net Pay	294.87 ————————	Actual amount received (C) A − B = C

Payee The person to whom a cheque is made payable, i.e. the person who is to receive payment.

Paying in Slip (See Credit Slip)

Payment by Results Wage payment that depends on the amount produced by the individual or team.

Payment Default   When a debtor has not paid an outstanding debt when due.

Payment in Kind   A reward given in exchange for work but not in the form of money, for example, use of a company car.

PC   Personal computer.

Pedlars   Traders who carry their wares from door-to-door on foot.

Penalty Clause   A condition contained in a contract stipulating a deduction in price to be paid if work, or some other commitment, is not completed by a certain time or to a certain specification.

Pending   Work or decision which is outstanding or undecided.

Pension Funds   The regular contributions which pension organisations collect from members to provide them with a pension when they retire. The contributions are made to work by investing in low-risk securities. When the organisers of such funds invest in this way they are sometimes referred to as 'institutional investors'.

Peppercorn Rent   A rent that is very low or nominal.

PEPS   Personal Equity Plans. The PEPS scheme aims to make it more attractive and simple for people, particularly small savers and first-time share-buyers, to invest in UK equities. The scheme allows people to invest a monthly or yearly amount, within a maximum defined by the Government, in shares entirely free of tax.

Perfect Competition/Perfect Market   A market in which there are many buyers and sellers, and none of these is large enough to influence the price. In such a perfect situation the price which is charged is determined by the interaction between consumers and the most effective of the sellers. In a perfect market all buyers and sellers have perfect knowledge of the market.

Perishable   Good which are liable to rot or wither, for example, food

Perpetual Inventory   A stocktaking technique undertaken by large organisations whereby a small section of stock is chosen at random and at regular intervals and checked carefully against stock records in a continual search for discrepancies.

Per Pro (p.p.)   An abbreviation of per procurationem meaning 'for and on behalf of'. It is used when authority has been delegated for one person to act in the capacity of another, for example, to sign a letter on behalf of another.

Personal Loan   A loan to an individual as opposed to a business loan.

Personnel Department   A department in a firm which is concerned with finding the right person for vacant jobs, and if necessary giving them induction training. This department also deals with resignations, providing testimonials and dismissing unsuitable workers. It maintains personal records of all employees and is involved in the welfare and happiness of all personnel.

Percentage Profit   A profit calculated by:

$$\frac{\text{profit}}{\text{turnover}} \times 100$$

Personal Allowances   The tax relief given according to a person's individual responsibilities and circumstances.

Person to Person   A telephone call service in which the operator calls the person whom the caller wishes to talk to, and the charges are only calculated from the time when the caller and the person being contacted are connected.

Persuasive Adverstising   A form of advertising which aims to persuade people to buy a product whether they need the item or not, and tries to relate the product to some hidden persuader, for example, the desire to be popular or 'trendy'.

Petty Cash   A sum of money set aside by a business for payment of small amounts of expenses.

Petty Cash Voucher   A note replacing a receipt when the amount of expenditure concerned is small and receipts are not readily available, for example, bus fare.

PETTY CASH VOUCHER

AUTHORISED BY	RECEIVED BY	AMOUNT	
J. Harris	Sarah Hicks		
DATE	DESCRIPTION	£	p
2/8/19-	Taxi to station	5	00
	TOTAL	5	00

PETTY CASH VOUCHER

AUTHORISED BY	RECEIVED BY	AMOUNT	
H. Roberts	A N Jones		
DATE	DESCRIPTION	£	p
10/10/9	Paper clips		90
	Staples		50
	10 Ballpoint pens	1	00
	TOTAL	3	40

Physical Barriers   Obstacles to the free movement of people and goods between EC Member States. These include customs and immigration posts and border checks on health and safety of goods. Abolition of physical barriers implies common policies for all Member States on matters such as drugs, terrorism, visas, immigration from outside the EC, firearms, extradition and animal health.

Picketing   A group of striking workers may stand outside a firm's entrance to try to persuade other workers not to 'cross the picket line', i.e. not to enter the premises in order to maximise the effect of their industrial action. (See also Secondary Picket)

Pictogram/Pictograph   A picture or symbol standing for a word or group of words. Often used in the presentation of statistics to make them more interesting.

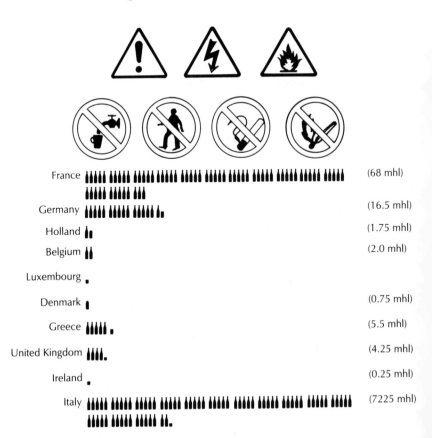

Piecework   A method a wage payment which is calculated in relation to the number of items produced by an individual or a group of workers.

Pie Chart   A circular graph divided into sectors proportional to the relative size of the quantities represented. It is the simplest picture that can be made from numbers. It should only be used when there are six or less segments, otherwise the information conveyed can appear too confusing.

$$\text{Bus} \quad 12\tfrac{12}{30} \times \tfrac{360}{1} = 144°$$

$$\text{Walk} \quad 13\tfrac{13}{30} \times \tfrac{360}{1} = 156°$$

$$\text{Bicycle} \quad 5\tfrac{3}{30} \times \tfrac{360}{1} = 60°$$

$$\text{Total} \quad 30 \qquad 360°$$

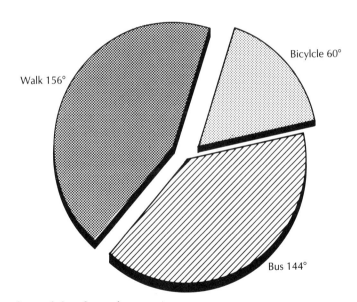

A pie chart of the above data

Pilferage   The loss through theft, for example, from supermarket shelves, or from goods in transit.

PIN   Personal Identification Number. A unique number allocated to a cash card holder which must be keyed into the cash dispenser in order to obtain cash or access to other machine services.

Pipe, The   Information network being set up by the members of the Federation of Stock Exchanges to provide access on-screen to prices in other European Community countries.

PKG   Abbreviation of packing or packaging.

Plaintiff   A person who brings a civil action in a court of law.

Planned Economy (Command Economy)   An economy where the state makes the major economic decisions. It decides how much of each good or service will be provided and then sets quotas for firms to ensure that the appropriate amount is produced.

PLC   (See Public Limited Company)

Plotter   An item of computer hardware that translates information into graphical or pictorial form onto paper or similar medium.

Plough Back   Putting profits back into a business by using them to buy new equipment.

Point of Order   An interruption to a meeting by one of those present to draw the attention of the Chairperson to some irregularity in the proceedings.

Point of Sale Advertising   The display advertising at the place where goods are actually sold, for example, shop counter displays, etc.

Point of Sale Terminal (POS)   A computerised till at a checkout position of a supermarket. Such a terminal can incorporate a bar code reader and may automatically update stock records as merchandise is taken from the store by customers.

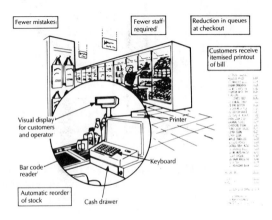

Policy   The document setting out the terms of the contract between the insurer (insurance company) and the insured.

Pooling of Risks   The principle of insurance whereby risks are 'shared', 'spread' or 'pooled' by those who contribute to an insurance pool.

POP Envelopes   The standard sizes of envelopes in the UK which the Post Office prefer and which help the mechanised handling of mail. (POP – Post Office Preferred).

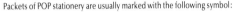

Packets of POP stationery are usually marked with the following symbol:

To fall within the POP range, envelopes must be:–

a no more than 6mm (¼") thick;
b at least 90mm × 140mm (3½" × 5½") and not larger than 120mm × 235mm (4¾" × 9¼");
c oblong in shape with the longer side at least 1·4 times the shorter;
d made from paper weighing at least 63 grammes per sq. metre.

The most widely used International Standards Organisation envelope sizes – DL and C6 are within the POP range, and measure 220mm × 110mm (4¼" × 8⅝") and 114mm × 162mm (4½" × 6⅜") respectively.

Port   A terminal or town where cargo or passengers have access to ships. An efficient port has to enable ships to 'turn round' quickly. The following are the main requirements of a modern port:

- Clear access channel with deep water
- Some protection from rough seas
- Wharves with appropriate lifting gear and equipment
- Warehouses, including specialist storage spaces
- Supplies of oil, water, and other ship's requirements
- Repair facilities such as dry dock
- Customs and immigration facilities
- Good links with road and rail network
- Buildings for offices and commercial services

Portfolio   A term referring to the sum of all assets invested in shares, bonds, debentures, deposits or other liquid income-bearing assets.

Postal Communication   A range of services provided by the Post Office in the UK which enables letters and parcels to be sent from one person or business to another.

Post Code   A series of letters and numbers included at the end of an address and used in the UK to assist in the mechanical sorting of mail. In some other countries the code is referred to as the Zip Code.

Post-Dated   A term which refers to cheques or other documents on which is written a date in the future. Payment against such items are not released until the date on the face of the document.

Poste Restante   A postal service by which packets may be sent to a post office in a particular town 'to be called for'. The Post Office keeps the packet for up to two weeks and only releases it upon proof of identity. The service is particularly useful to sales representatives or similar workers who are unsure where they will be residing during a sales tour.

Poundage   The commission charged by the Post Office on the purchase of postal orders. The amount charged varies with the value of the order.

Power of Attorney   Legal document giving one person the authority to act on behalf of another, for example, to sign cheques.

PR   Public relations. The practice of promoting, creating and maintaining goodwill and a favourable image of an organisation with the public.

Precedent   A decision or ruling that is subsequently taken as guidance for similar situations.

Precinct   A specially designed car-free shopping area for pedestrians.

Predatory Pricing   When an enterprise lowers its prices below cost in order to drive its competitors out of the market, with the intention of raising prices again later when the competition has been eliminated. Predatory pricing is prohibited by the EC Competition Policy.

Preference Share   Shares which have a priority claim on the profits of a company after debenture holders. Preference shares pay a fixed rate of dividend but only if sufficient profits are available to make the payment. Preference shares usually carry no voting rights.

Premium   The fee charged by an insurance company for covering a risk. The term is also used to refer to the profit on sale of shares.

Premium Savings Bonds   Bonds issued by the Treasury for purchase by the public. No interest is paid but there is a monthly draw for cash prizes of various sums.

Pre-Payment   Making payment in advance of when it is due.

President   A President is the European equivalent of a Chairman in the UK. The European Commission has a President chosen by the Member States. The European Parliament elects its own President, and the Community as a whole has a rotating 'Presidency'.

Pressure Groups   Voluntary organisations which seek to encourage the Government, council, or some other organisation to recognise their views and respond to them. They try to influence the decision-making process by demonstrating the strength of their feelings. Trade unions are one of the most well-known pressure groups in Britain, but there are many others such as the Consumers' Association which does much to help and guide consumers as well as protect their interests.

Prestel   Prestel is a two-way computerised information service. The service can be used by anyone who has a specially adapted television set and a telephone. The telephone connection is used to obtain up-to-the-minute news and information from an extensive data bank for display on the television screen. The Prestel service can respond to questions presented to it through a computer keyboard. For example, the data bank can be asked about road conditions; availability of air or theatre tickets; and bookings can be placed and accepted through the system.

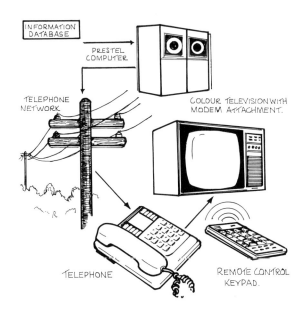

Pre-Tax Profit   The profit of an organisation prior to payment of any tax due, for example, corporation tax.

Price Leader   (See Loss Leader)

Prices Acts 1974 and 1975   Acts of the UK Parliament which gave the government the power to:
- Subsidise food
- Regulate food prices
- Require shopkeepers to display prices in a way that does not give a false impression.

Price Variance   The alterations caused by a change in the price of materials or labour.

Price War   A period of intense competition among enterprises in the same market, and characterised by repeated price reductions. A price war is sometimes deliberately instituted to drive competitors out of the market.

Primary Production   The first stage in the process of production in which products are produced or extracted in their original form, for example, farming, fishing and mining.

Principal   The person who instructs a broker to help buy or sell goods.

Principle of Indemnity   (See Insurance)

Print-Out   Output of computer information printed on paper.

Private Limited Company   Any company which is not registered as a public limited company is a private company. This type of business must include Limited (or Ltd) in its title name. Such a company is allowed to have from two or more members (shareholders). The capital of the firm is divided into shares, but the shares are not sold on The Stock Exchange and they cannot be advertised for sale publicly. Consequently, shares have to be sold privately – hence the name 'private' company. (See also Public Limited Company)

Private Treaty   The situation when two people agree on a contract of sale privately, without the goods being offered openly on the market.

Privatisation Transfer of ownership of a State-owned enterprise (public enterprise) to the private sector of ownership, e.g., British Telecom and British Gas.

PRO Public relations officer. A management employee with the responsibility of trying to ensure that the public has a favourable impression of the company.

Problem Regions (Depressed Areas) Regions of the country or the European Community where there is high unemployment and where industry has declined.

Producer A person or organisation that makes or grows something.

Producers' Co-operative An organisation formed by producers to buy raw materials or sell products.

Product Development The early stages of producing something when the decision has to be taken whether it is worthwhile to pursue a new project.

Production Quotas Limits on the amount of a particularly commodity which farmers are allowed to produce, for example, milk quotas.

Product Liability The EC Product Liability Directive makes manufacturers strictly liable for any injuries caused by their defective products. It was implemented in the UK in the 1987 Consumer Protection Act.

Product Life Cycle All products move through identifiable stages which are referred to as the 'product life cycle'. Understanding this cycle assists the preparation of a sound marketing plan.

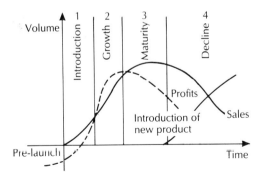

Product life cycle

Product Mix   (See Product Range and Mix)

Product Range and Mix   Most products are not marketed on their own but are part of a range of products. For example, a firm might produce a range of cake mixes; chocolate, coconut, orange, lemon. A large firm will not only have a product range but will also have a 'product mix' which consists of several different products, each with its own range, for example, cakes, biscuits, crisps, etc.

Productivity   Producing goods or services.

Productivity Agreement   An agreement reached between an employer and workers or their representatives to attempt to achieve certain levels of output.

Professional Associations   Associations set up by many trades and professions to formulate and administer Codes of Practice which include procedures for dealing with consumer complaints.

Profit   The reward the entrepreneur receives for taking the risk involved in business and for being able to combine all the factors required to produce and sell goods or services. (See also Gross Profit and Net Profit)

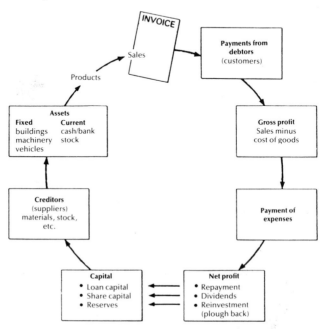

Profit and Loss Account   A financial statement showing the profits and losses made by a firm over a period of time.

Profit Margin   Profit margin is the percentage of the selling price which is the seller's profit. For example, on an article with a cost price of 80p which is sold for £1 the profit margin is:

$$\frac{20}{100} \times 100 = 20\%$$

(See also Mark-Up)

Pro-Forma Invoice   An invoice which is issued for the sake of formality (in form only). It is similar to an invoice but only used in special circumstances such as when payment is required before goods are sent and when the goods are to be inspected first by the buyer.

Program   A series of instructions written in a form that a computer can understand.

Programmer   A person who writes computer programs.

Progress Chaser   A supervisory worker employed to ensure that delivery schedules are adhered to. They will not only ensure that goods are produced in their employer's factory on time, but will also have the responsibility of making sure that suppliers deliver raw materials to the factory in time for requirements.

Progressive Tax   A tax where the proportion taken in tax rises as income rises; it takes a larger proportion of income from higher income groups. Income Tax is a progressive tax.

Promissory Note   An unconditional promise, in writing, made by one person, and signed by them, to pay a sum of money at a certain time to another person.

Promoter   A person (or group) who helps to organise, develop, or finance an undertaking such as a company or activity/project.

Promotion   (See Sales Promotion)

Promotion Expense   An expense incurred in the formation of a new enterprise or activity.

Proprietorship   A single owner of a business.

Prompt Cash   The payment of goods soon after they are delivered to the buyer

Proposal Form   (See Insurance)

Proposer   A person seeking insurance cover.

Pro Rata   In proportion.

Prospectus   A document which is issued when an invitation is made to the public to subscribe to shares in a company. It includes details of the company's accounts for previous years and a forecast of profits, and must comply with the relevant provisions of the Companies Acts. (See also Insurance)

Protectionist Measures   Measures such as tariffs and quotas used by a country to restrict imports and protect domestic industries from foreign competition.

Proximate Cause   (See Insurance)

Proxy   A person empowered by someone to act on their behalf, for example, to vote at a meeting. The authority is usually signified in writing.

Proxy Card   The form supplied by a company by which a shareholder can appoint a proxy to act on their behalf at the company's meeting.

Public Corporation   A business with limited liability, owned by the Government but run independently and expected to be self-financing, current examples are The British Broadcasting Corporation and British Rail.

Public Enterprise   Businesses operated by local or central government.

- Municipal undertakings are businesses or services operated on a commercial basis by local government, for example, local transport, libraries, swimming pools, banqueting halls, etc.
- State undertakings are businesses operated by central government on behalf of the public.

The amount of public enterprise in the economy is often dependent upon political views.

Public Expenditure   Government spending.

Public Limited Company (plc)   A company which can offer its shares for sale to the general public on the open market and whose shares are listed on The Stock Exchange. The public limited company must indicate its public status by including the letters PLC (public limited company) in its title name. When an investor buys shares in a PLC they become a part-owner. This not only entitles them to a share of the company's profits, but also gives them the right to some say in the way that the company is operated. It is usual for the shareholders of a company to elect a small committee called a Board of Directors to decide on overall company policy on behalf of the shareholders. A chairperson is also elected regulate board meetings. The board of directors is too large a group of people for all of them to take an active part in the day-to-day operation of the firm so the board appoint a Managing Director to carry out this function. (See also Private Limited Company)

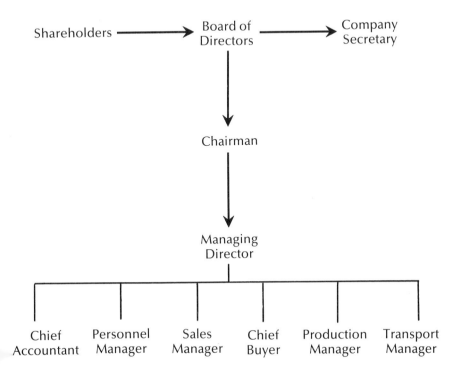

Public Notary   A public officer, usually a solicitor, authorised to administer oaths, draw up and attest documents, etc.

Public Procurement   Purchases by public bodies, including utilities and national and local government.

Public Sector Borrowing Requirement (PSBR)   The amount that the Government has to borrow when public sector spending is higher than what it has gained through taxation.

Pyramid Selling   A practice adopted by some manufacturers of advertising for distributors and selling them batches of goods. The first distributors then advertise for more distributors who are sold sub-divisions of the original batches at an increased price. This process continues until the final distributors are left with stock that may be unsellable except at a loss.

Qualification   An ability, quality, or attribute, that fits a person to perform a particular job or task.

Quality Control   A type of policy and procedure used to maintain a desired level of standards in operations or production.

Quango   Quasi-autonomous national government organisation or quasi-autonomous non-governmental organisation. A semi-independent body set up by the Government to meet functions decided by the Government, for example, the British Medical Council, Monopolies and Mergers Commission, tourist boards and consumer councils.

Quantitive Ingredient Declaration (QUID)   Legislation proposed by the EC which will require producers to declare on food labels the quantity of the main or characterising ingredients as a percentage of the whole, rather than just listing the ingredients in declining order of volume as at present.

Quantity Allowance   A reduction in price allowed for purchase of large quantities.

Quasi   Resembling but not actually. A situation which has close similarity to reality.

Quick Assets   Resources which are rapidly available such as cash debtors, stock, etc.

Quiet Possession   After goods are sold, the seller gives up all claims to the goods and the buyer may do as they wish with them.

Quorum   A minimum number of members in an assembly, society, board of directors, etc., required to be present before any valid business can be transacted.

Quota   A limit set by an importing country on the amount of a certain type of product which can be imported into that country from a specified other country.

Quota Brokers   Brokers who help traders with unused surplus quotas to sell them to other traders who may want to make use of them.

Quota Licence   A document giving an importer permission to bring a specific quantity of a particular type of product into the country.

Quotation, for Goods   The price and terms upon which a supplier is willing to undertake an order.

Quotation, Stock Exchange   The double price given in through the Stock Exchange quotation system.

Quoted Company   An out-dated term for a listed company – a company whose shares are listed on The Stock Exchange.

Race Relations Act 1976   An Act of the UK Parliament which forbids discrimination on racial grounds. It is supported by the Commission for Racial Equality which was also set up under the Act to enforce the legislation and to promote racial equality.

Rack Rent   The maximum rent that can be obtained for a particular property.

Rally   A recovery in prices, for example, shares, commodities, etc.

RAM   Random access memory. RAM is a temporary memory in a computer. RAM is lost when the computer is switched off.

Random Sample   A grouping in which all of the elements have been drawn arbitarily.

Rapid Notification System   An EC system whereby Member States warn the Commission's Consumer Policy Service about any dangerous products they become aware of. The Commission then warns other Member States.

Rate   A price for a service for a specific unit of time, for example, a consultation rate of £50 per hour.

Rate of Exchange   The price at which one currency is sold or exchanged for another.

Rate of Return   The actual return or annual percentage return on the amount of money invested.

Rate of Stock Turnover   A measure of the speed at which stock is turned over in a year. It is calculated by:

$$\frac{\text{cost of stock sold}}{\text{cost of average stock}} = \text{rate of stock turnover}$$

The value of average stock is worked out by taking the stock value at the beginning and at the end of the trading period, adding them and dividing by two.

Ratification   To give formal approval or consent.

Ratio   The relationship of one amount to another.

Raw Material   Goods bought for use as all or part of a finished product. The term does not include supplies used in manufacturing that do not become part of the finished product.

Real Estate   Freehold land and buildings.

Rebate   An allowance, discount, or refund of part of the price paid for goods or services.

Receipt   A written note confirming that a certain sum of money or goods has been received by a specified person.

Receiver   A person appointed by a Court to manage property until the outcome of legal proceedings are known.

Receiving Order   An instruction by a Court transferring assets owned by a bankrupt into the hands of the Official Receiver.

Reception   The part of a firm concerned with receiving and monitoring visitors to the premises.

Recession   A temporary depression in economic activity. (See Business Cycle)

Recommended Resale Price   The guideline price suggested by the manufacturer. Discounts and reductions offered by retailers are based on this price.

Recorded Delivery   A service provided by the Post Office whereby they will obtain a signature upon delivery of a package.

Recoup   To regain or make good a financial loss.

Recovery Value   Estimated income from resale or scrapping of a fixed asset.

Recruitment   The process of obtaining new employees, mainly carried out by the Personnel Department in a large organisation.

Redeemable Bonds   Securities that are payable at par on a certain date.

Redeemable Shares   Shares that a company may buy back from its shareholders.

Redemption Period   The period during which an item pawned is redeemable.

Redemption Yield   A calculation which takes into consideration not only the interest which will become payable on an amount of stock but also the capital profit which will be obtained when the stock is redeemed. The figure is expressed on an annual basis.

Red Tape   Obstructive official routine or procedure; time-consuming bureaucracy.

Redundancy   A situation when an employee loses their job because it no longer exists. This may occur because the business has been forced to cease trading, or when the firm no longer needs the same number of workers. When an employee loses their job as a result of redundancy they need financial help to enable them to make the transition to new employment. The Redundancies Payments Act in the UK requires employers to make a lump sum payment to employees being made redundant (so long as they have served a minimum period of time, and are aged 18 or over). The amount of redundancy compensation depends upon the age, length of service, and pay of the employee.

Redundancy Payments Act   (See Redundancy)

Redundant   Surplus to requirements.

Re-Export   Goods imported, stored in an area supervised by Customs and later sold to another country. Re-exporting is also known as the entrepôt trade. (See also Entrepôt Trade)

Referee   A person who provides a reference or character assessment for someone, usually when that person is looking for a job.

Reference   A supporting statement on somebody's character and trustworthiness.

Refer to Drawer (RD)   The words or letters written on a cheque which the bank, for some reason, has declined to pass for payment. The message is to the payee telling them they must find out from the drawer the reason why payment has been refused.

Reflation   An attempt by the Government to increase economic activity.

Refund   An amount paid back to a purchaser, either in cash or as a credit allowance.

Registered Capital   The amount of money that a company is allowed to raise from its owners. This is also referred to as authorised capital or nominal capital.

Registered Office   The official address of a company and to where all important communications should be sent.

Registered Post   A Post Office service in the UK for the delivery of packets containing items of value, and for which compensation is paid if loss occurs.

Registered Trade Mark   A trade mark which has been registered with the appropriate authorities in the country to which the mark applies.

Registrar   Official having responsibility for maintaining official records, for example, Registrar of Companies.

Registrar of Companies   Government official with whom all forming companies must register.

Re-Insurance   The transfer of insurance risk from one insurance company to another in order to spread the risk.

Release A document freeing a person from an obligation.

Remittance The payment for goods or services.

Remittance Advice Note A note which should accompany any payment to state what the payment is for.

Remote Access Access gained to a computer through a terminal sited away from the central processing unit.

Remuneration The wage, salary or other reward given for work or service carried out by an employee for an employer.

Rendu A price quotation for goods which includes their delivery to the buyer's premises in a foreign country.

Rent A payment made periodically by a tenant to a landlord or owner for the occupation or use of land, buildings or other property, such as a telephone.

Representative Person acting on behalf of another, for example, a sales person.

Reprography The art or process of copying, reprinting, or reproducing printed material.

Reputable Of good reputation.

Requisition An official form which contains details of an internal demand for supplies.

Resale Prices Act 1964 An Act of the UK Parliament which helps to protect consumers by enforcing the following rules:

- Suppliers are not allowed to impose a minimum price at which their goods must be sold, but they can suggest a manufacturers recommended price (MRP).
- Suppliers cannot refuse supplies to a retailer who sells below the recommended price
- Books, maps and medicines are exempt from this Act.

Rescind To annul, repeal or cancel.

Reserve A part of the profits of a business retained to meet unexpected demands.

Reserve Price   The lowest price that a person is willing to accept for their goods when being sold by public auction, and the reserve figure ensures that the item is not sold too cheaply.

Restrictive Practices   Practices which are the methods or weapons used by the unions in an industrial dispute. These include: strikes – official and unofficial, demarcation disputes ('who does what'), overtime ban, working to rule, go slow, closed shop (only working with people of same union), picketing, sit-in (refusing to leave premises), and blacking (refusing to work on or move certain equipment).

Restrictive Trade Practices Act 1976   An Act of the UK Parliament which aims to safeguard the consumer against the practice of agreements between companies to limit production or supply in order to keep prices artificially high, and to exploit a monopolistic position.

Retailer   A trader who sells goods to consumers who are the final users of the goods.

Retail Price   The price at which a retailer sells their goods to consumers.

Retail Price Index (RPI)   An index of retail prices based on the Government assessment of current prices in comparison with a base year assessed as 100. See the page opposite.

Retainer   A fee paid to a person in advance to secure the first option to call on their services with agreed terms and conditions.

Return on Capital Invested   The proprietor's rewards on the money they have invested, i.e. the return on capital invested. This figure is very important to the businessperson because it shows how much profit has been made as a percentage of the capital originally put into the business. The return on the investment must be sufficient to make it worthwhile for the owners of the business to face the risks involved. If the return is not sufficient the owner(s) may be tempted to place their money in other less risky forms of investment. The return on capital invested is calculated as follows:

$$\text{Return on capital invested} = \frac{\text{Net profit}}{\text{Capital at start of year}} \times 100$$

Revenue   The current income from an organisation for a given period

Revenue 167

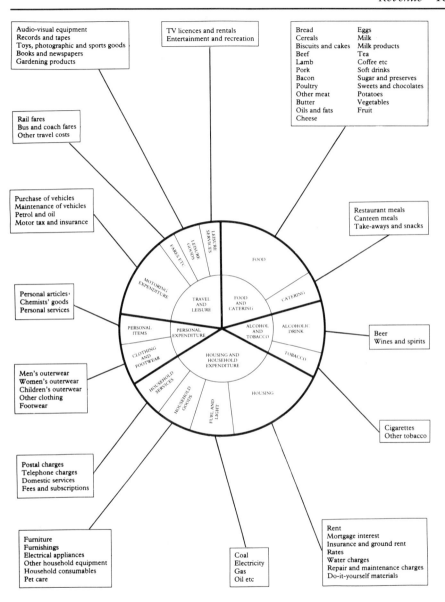

Structure of the RPI

Revocable Letter of Credit   A letter of credit which can be cancelled by the issuing bank or the accountee at any time without notice.

Rider   An additional clause or amendment to a legal document.

Rights Issue   An offer to take up new shares in a company which is only addressed to existing shareholders. This is a means by which an existing company can raise additional capital.

Ring   A group or organisation of people, usually illegal, co-operating for the self-interested purpose of controlling a market in order to obtain property at a price well below the true market value and to share the profit gained.

Roll On, Roll Off Ferries   Specially built ships that allow vehicles to drive on and off.

Roll Over   To continue lending or borrowing money, usually for a limited period, after the original arrangement was intended to end. A new rate of interest is usually negotiated.

ROM   Read only memory. Computer memory which can be used but not altered. Programs kept in ROM include the operating system and sometimes the language the computer uses.

Royal Mint   The Government Department in the UK having sole responsibility for production of coins for circulation.

Royalty   A sum of money paid for the right to use another person's property or work, for example, a percentage of the revenue from the sale of a book, performance of a theatrical work, or use of a patented invention, etc.

Safe Deposit Box   A secure box kept in the bank's vault for the safekeeping of customer's valuables, important documents, etc.

Safeguard Clause   An EC rule which allows a Member country to introduce import controls if sudden surges in the volume of imports damage its home industry.

Salary   A fixed regular payment made by an employer, often monthly usually for professional or office work as opposed to manual work.

Sale-and-Lease Back   The sale of business assets (for example, land buildings or equipment) which is then leased back to the firm so tha they can continue to use it. The aim of the deal is to enable the business to gain access to additional cash flow in exchange for assets.

Sale of Goods Act 1979   An Act of the UK Parliament which covers all goods (including food) bought from a trader through a shop, doorstep seller, or sales by mail order. The seller has three main obligations. Goods must:

1) Be of 'merchantable quality'. This means that goods must be reasonably fit for their normal purpose, bearing in mind the price paid, the nature of the goods, and how they were described. Thus a new item must not be damaged and it must work properly

2) Be 'as described'. They must correspond with the description given by the seller, or in accordance with labels on the item or the packing

3) Be 'fit for any particular purpose made known to the seller'. If you ask for plates that are 'dishwasher safe', and the seller assures you that they are, he has broken his contract with you if they are not.

Sales Department   A department in a large firm especially for the marketing of the firms goods or services. Such a department will plan an organise the selling of goods or services offered by the firm. This department is one of the most essential because without it other departments would not be needed.

Sales Promotion   Inducements to encourage further purchases of a product, for example, free gifts, free samples, etc.

Sales Representative   A person employed to provide an important link between a company and its existing and potential customers.

Sale or Return   An arrangement whereby goods are sold on the basis that if they are not used or sold within a given period of time the buyer may return them without incurring payment.

Salvage   Property saved from fire or some other disaster.

Sample   A small portion of a larger part which serves to represent the typical standard or quality of the whole.

Save as You Earn (SAYE)   A saving scheme promoted by the UK Government whereby contributions to the scheme by savers are deducted from pay with each wage payment under a contract arrangement.

Savings Account   An account in which savers can deposit money in a bank and withdraw their deposits at any time. Interest is received on amounts deposited.

Scale of Preference   Putting wants into an order of priority.

Screwdriver Plants   Plants set up within the EC by non-EC manufacturers where the local workforce is employed to assemble imported components.

Scrip Issue   Issue of shares free to existing shareholders in proportion to the number of shares they already hold.

SEAQ   Stock Exchange Automated Quotation System. (See Market Makers)

Secondary Picket   A picket mounted by workers at a place other than that where they are employed. (See also Picketing)

Secondary Production   The second stage of production in which the raw materials extracted from primary production are processed and transformed into finished products.

- Manufacturers may be involved in the production of a complete item, or they may make parts which will be assembled into a finished article.
- Construction industries take raw materials and partly finished products and change them into buildings, roads and bridges, etc.

Second Mortgage   A loan raised on the security provided by property that is already the subject of a loan or mortgage.

Secretary-General   The head of the staff of the European Commission. The Council of Ministers is also supported by a staff headed by a Secretary General.

Secured Debenture   A fixed debenture that is secured against certain fixed assets of a company; if the company cannot repay its debt or interest on the debenture then the debenture holder can take charge of the asset.

Securities   'Securities' is the collective term for Stocks and Shares in common usage. These and other securities, such as house deeds and insurance policies are sometimes lodged with banks, etc., as collateral against loans.

Selectapost A Post Office service in the UK whereby an addressee's mail is subdivided (for example, into departments) prior to delivery so long as some indication of the division required is shown on the envelope. This makes the internal distribution easier.

Self-Service Stores Shops where customers collect goods from shelves themselves and leave the store through a checkout station, for example, a supermarket.

Selective Distribution Agreements The arrangements under which the distribution of products is confined to dealers who may have specialised expertise and facilities, for example, agreements between motor manufacturers and car dealers.

Sequestration The placing of some disputed property in the hands of a third person pending settlement of a dispute.

Sequestrator The person with responsibility for sequestered property.

Set Aside An EC agreement that EC Member States can pay farmers to take land out of agricultural production, in an effort to reduce cereal supluses.

Settlement The payment of an outstanding debt or claim.

Settlement Day The last day for settling debts in a Stock Exchange 'account' or trading period.

Sex Discrimination Act 1975 An Act of the UK Parliament which makes discrimination on grounds of sex unlawful in employment and education.

Share Certificates of ownership in a company which entitle the holder to dividends and voting rights in the company's election of directors. See page 172.

Share Capital The amount of shares authorised for issue by a company's Memorandum of Association.

Shareholder The holder of a share certificate showing part-ownership of a limited company.

Shares (See Ordinary Share)

No. of Certificate	Transfer No (s)		Date of Registration	No. of Shares
1423			1 DEC 2005	2000

ORDINARY SHARES

Bailey Marine plc
(Incorporated in England under the Companies Act 1948–1980)

This is to Certify that MISS ANN BUYER 94 THE CRESCENT HORSHAM WEST SUSSEX RH13 1NB

	HUNDREDS OF THOUSANDS	TENS OF THOUSANDS	THOUSANDS	HUNDREDS	TENS	UNITS
is/are the Registered Holder(s) of			TWO	—	—	—

ORDINARY SHARES of fifty pence each, fully paid, in **BAILEY MARINE plc**, subject
to the Memorandum and Articles of Association of the Company.

Given under the Common Seal of the Company

Note: No transfer of any of the Ordinary Shares comprised in this Certificate will be registered until this Certificate has been lodged with the Registrars

Share Certificate

Shift System   The organisation of working hours into blocks of time so that one group of workers can be followed by another.

Shipping Agent   A company which specialises in deciding the best form of transport and arranging the necessary documentation. It can also be referred to as a freight forwarding agent.

Shop Floor   The area of the factory where production takes place.

Shop Lifter   A person who steals goods from shops during shopping hours.

Shopping Centre   An area in a town where most of the shops are sited.

Shopping Precincts   (See Precincts)

Shop Soiled   Items that have been on display in a shop and as a result have become faded, worn or tarnished.

Shop Steward   An elected representative of the union workers in shop, factory, etc.

Short-Dated Securities ('Shorts')   Loans made by investors to organisations and due to be repaid at a specific date. A short-dated security only has a short time to run before their maturity date. In the case of government securities the term applies where the maturity date is less than five years.

Shrinkage   A term used in stock control, especially in the retail trade, to refer to unexplained loss of stock (for example, pilferage).

Silent Partner   A partner who is publicly known to be a member of a firm but is not active in the management of it. (See also Partnership)

Single European Market   The European Community aims to create a common unified market within the Community boundaries – an internal market.

Single Use Goods   Goods that are used only once only.

Sit-In   A form of industrial action where workers occupy their employer's premises ensuring that no goods enter or leave, and preventing the operation of the firm. Sometimes, such as when a factory is threatened with closure, the sit-in becomes a 'work-in'. Workers occupy the factory and keep it in operation without the presence of the management.

Sleeping Partner   (See Partnership)

Slow Moving Stock   Stocks which are not sold easily. It may be that the price is unrealistic, marketing techniques such as advertising or display may be inappropriate, the quality poor, or the product is out of fashion.

Slump   A continuing fall in economic activity, evident in falling market demand and market prices. (See also Business Cycle)

Slush Fund   A fund used for making secret payments in return for favours, or anticipated favours.

Snake   A term used to refer to a system of currency exchange by a group of countries (for example, EC Member States), whereby the national currencies are linked together in such a way that a change in the exchange rate of one will affect all the others.

Software   The programs, or group of programs, which control the hardware of a computer.

Social Dumping   The situation where firms in the EC may tend to move jobs to Member States with the weakest labour protection, lowest wages, and cheapest employers' social security contributions.

Social Security, Department of A department of the UK government which is responsible for the provision of social services such as National Insurance, family benefit, supplementary benefits and war pensions.

Sole Agent A wholesaler or retailer who is given exclusive rights by a manufacturer to sell goods in a particular region. This means that they are the only agent through which other dealers can obtain these goods.

Sole Proprietorship/Sole Trader A business owned by only one person. A major disadvantage of such a business that it lacks limited liability and a separate corporate identity.

Solvency The ability of a company to pay its debts when they become due.

Space Buyers Agents acting for clients attempting to buy suitable display space for advertising.

Span of Control The number of subordinates a manager supervises, or the effective limit to the number of others that a manager can supervise effectively.

Special Deposits The deposits which may have to be made by the commercial banks at the Bank of England on its orders, and which are frozen until further notice. The aim of such action is to withdraw money from the economy as a part of monetary policy.

Specialisation (See Division of Labour)

Speculation A quick profit made by anticipating changes in prices (for example, of commodities or shares).

Spot Cash The buying of goods by paying for them immediately.

Spot Deal A contract to buy or sell something where the transaction is to take place immediately.

Spot Price The current daily price for a deal 'on the spot'.

Spreadsheets A computer software package that allows the computer operator to enter, store and analyse data in columns and rows of figures VDU screen. This data can be printed out as a whole or in part.

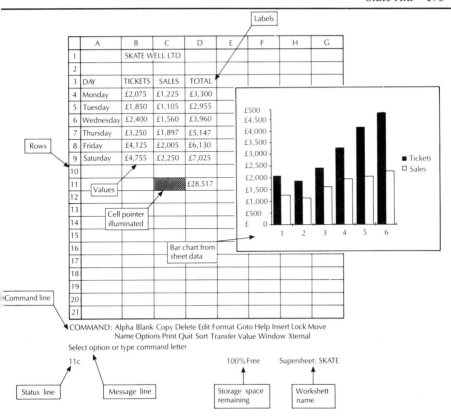

Stags Speculators who buy new share issues in the expectation that they can be sold for a higher price when they are traded on The Stock Exchange.

Stale Cheque A cheque which is more than six months old. Banks will not accept such a cheque and the holder must refer to the drawer for payment.

Standing Order An order given by the account holder instructing their bank to transfer a certain sum of money to another account at regular intervals.

State Aid Direct or indirect subsidies by EC Member States to home industries. They may take the form of grants, cheap loans and tax concessions. Member States have to notify these to the Commission. They can lead to artificial price levels which distort free competition within the Community.

Statement of Account A statement summarising a firm's accounts within a given period and giving the balance or amount due.

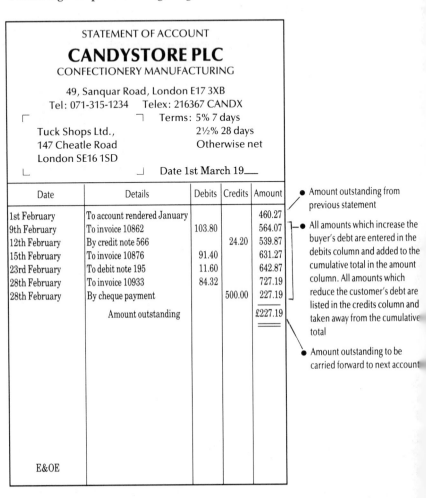

STATEMENT OF ACCOUNT

CANDYSTORE PLC

CONFECTIONERY MANUFACTURING

49, Sanquar Road, London E17 3XB
Tel: 071-315-1234   Telex: 216367 CANDX

Terms: 5% 7 days
2½% 28 days
Otherwise net

Tuck Shops Ltd.,
147 Cheatle Road
London SE16 1SD

Date 1st March 19___

Date	Details	Debits	Credits	Amount	
1st February	To account rendered January			460.27	● Amount outstanding from previous statement
9th February	To invoice 10862	103.80		564.07	●— All amounts which increase the buyer's debt are entered in the debits column and added to the cumulative total in the amount column. All amounts which reduce the customer's debt are listed in the credits column and taken away from the cumulative total
12th February	By credit note 566		24.20	539.87	
15th February	To invoice 10876	91.40		631.27	
23rd February	To debit note 195	11.60		642.87	
28th February	To invoice 10933	84.32		727.19	
28th February	By cheque payment		500.00	227.19	
	Amount outstanding			£227.19	● Amount outstanding to be carried forward to next account
E&OE					

Status Enquiry Agency A firm which specialises in obtaining and selling information about the financial situation and credit-worthiness of firms.

Sterling The UK currency, i.e. the pound sterling.

Stet A correction sign used in text editing to indicate that words crossed out are to remain as written.

Stock   1) Goods or materials kept by a firm in a special place called a warehouse, store or stock room, and held to be available when required against orders from customers or requisitions from internal departments.   2) Interest-bearing certificates which can be traded in a stock exchange. The term is generally applied to transferable securities issued by the Government, local authorities and companies.

Stock Control   (See Stocktaking)

Stock Exchange   A market in which second-hand securities can be bought and sold.

Stock Exchange Council   The council which controls the British Stock Exchange and is elected by the Members of The Stock Exchange. The Council has the following functions:

• Controls the admission of new Members
• Disciplines Members who are guilty of misconduct
• Formulates the Stock Exchange rules
• Settles disputes between Members
• Provides settlement and information services to Members.

Stock Market   A market in which new securities and second-hand securities can be bought and sold. The market is wider than just The Stock Exchange.

Stocktaking/Stock Control   The process of periodically checking stock on the shelves or in the warehouse to ensure that it is being looked after properly. This is carried out at least annually and sometimes more frequently, and is an important aspect of financial statements.

Stockturn   (See Stock Turnover)

Stop   An instruction given to a bank by an account holder to tell them not to pay a cheque when it is presented for payment. Such an instruction may incur a charge by the bank depending upon the reason for the 'stop' order.

Strike   Withdrawal of labour by a group of workers.

Subrogation, Principle of   A principle of insurance in which the insurer takes over the ownership and legal rights of a property if a total loss has occurred and the indemnity has been paid.

Subsidies   Assistance given, usually by the Government, in the form of finance towards the cost of a home-produced product to enable it to be sold at a lower price at home or abroad.

Superannuation   A pension payable on retirement.

Supermarket   A large retail shop of 18 square metres or more that mainly sells groceries and where the customers serve themselves and pay as they pass out of the shop through a checkout system with several till points.

Surrender Value   The amount of money that can be obtained from a life assurance policy if the policyholder surrenders it with no further claim on it.

Supply   The amount of a commodity that producers are willing to put on to the market at various prices in a given period of time. For each price the amount supplied is different. Alternatively, it could be said that the supply curve shows the price necessary to persuade the producer to provide output. Usually the higher the price the more of the commodity the producer will want to supply, although there are exceptions to this.

Market supply schedule	
Price	Quantity
10p	100
20p	200
30p	300
40p	400
50p	500

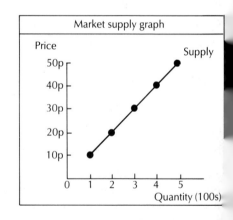

Market supply graph

Supply of Goods and Services Act 1982   An Act of the UK Parliament which applies the terms of the Sale of Goods Act to goods supplied as part of a service, for example, faulty taps provided by a plumber, and where goods are hired or exchanged instead of actually being purchased. The Act also provides that a person providing a service must do so:

• With reasonable skill and care

- Within reasonable time
- For a reasonable charge.

Support Price A general term used in relation to the EC to describe the various mechanisms of the Common Agricultural Policy which keep food prices up. They include 'threshhold prices' and 'target prices'.

Surety A person who is bound to be responsible for the performance of some duty undertaken by another.

Surface Mail The service operated by the Post Office in the UK which sends letters and parcels by ship or train to destinations abroad.

Surplus Goods Goods which are not consumed by their producer. The profits of a public enterprise or a co-operative are called a surplus because they are used for welfare or to benefit members and they are usually distributed.

Surrender Value The amount of money which an assurance company will pay to the assured or their assignees under the policy if the policy is given up and any claims extinguished.

Syndicate A group or partnership of underwriting members of Lloyd's of London (the UK central insurance market).

Syndicated Loan Loans which are so large that no single bank is willing or able to accept them are shared amongst several banks and financial institutions.

Sweat Shop A factory where employees work long hours for very low pay, and sometimes in poor conditions.

Swing The movement of a current account from debit to credit. When an overdraft limit is agreed a bank always wishes to see a swing in the figures. If the overdraft remains more or less close to the limit agreed it is said to be solid.

Switching The change from one currency to another or from one investment into another.

Systems Analysis The process of examining the way that a business is run with the aim of identifying ways in which efficiency can be improved. The person who carries out this highly specialised work is called a systems analyst.

TAC   (See Total Allowable Catch)

Tachograph   A device for producing a graphical record of its readings. It is particularly used to record the speed and distance covered by a heavy goods vehicle.

Take-Over   Where an outsider or another company takes control of a firm through purchase of at least 51 per cent of its shares, often without the agreement of the the directors of the firm being taken over. (See also Merger)

TALISMAN   The Stock Exchange's computerised settlement system. The letters stand for Transfer Accounting, Lodging for Investors and Stock Management.

Tangible Assets   (See Fixed Assets)

Tap Stocks   Government stocks which the Government Broker will supply at a given price. The price chosen, set in consultation with the Bank of England, provides a means of influencing interest rates in general. The complete issue is initially taken by the Bank of England who 'turn on the tap' by releasing the stock at the determined price.

Tare Weight   The weight of the packaging of an item.

Target Audience   The section of the population to whom an advertisement or product is intended to appeal.

Target Price   Target prices are set each year by the EC Council of Ministers as part of the Common Agricultural Policy. They represent the return that the Council wants farmers to receive on their sales.

Tariffs   These are a tax or custom duty imposed on imported goods to raise the price of foreign goods entering the country. There are two methods of imposing tariffs, which are collected by HM Customs and Excise Department:

1) Specific duties are a set price for each item imported.
2) Ad valorem duties are calculated as a percentage of the value of the imports.

Taxable Income   Income that is subject to government tax. After deducting various allowances due to a person, for example, dependents, the remainder is subject to taxation.

Taxation, Functions of   The primary function of taxation is to raise revenue to pay for those goods and services supplied by the State which private enterprise is usually unable or unwilling to provide at prices that the majority of the population are generally able to pay, for example, defence and education. Taxation can also be used to influence expenditure, to redistribute income, or to satisfy specific government objectives, for example, discouraging habits such as smoking, drinking and gambling, or encouraging other activities such as motivating industry to move into depressed areas.

Taxation, Principles of There are four basic principles of taxation. Taxes should be:

1) Based on the ability to pay
2) Collected as economically as possible
3) Operated by a system that is easy to understand
4) Relatively easy to collect.

Taxation, Types of Tax can be divided into two basic categories; direct taxes and indirect taxation.

1) **Direct Taxation** – a direct tax is one which is paid directly to the tax authority by the person against whom the tax is levied. Income tax, corporation tax, capital gains tax and capital transfer tax are examples.

2) **Indirect Taxation** – an indirect tax is paid by the taxpayer indirectly to the tax authority, i.e. levied on one person but is collected and ultimately paid by someone else such as a retailer, for example, value added tax.

Tax Code Number A code determined by the inspector of taxes in the UK from the claim for allowances made by a person liable to pay income tax. This number is notified to both the employer and the employee and is used to denote tax free pay allowed. (Notification of the tax code number is sent out by the tax office on Form P2).

Tax Tables Tables sent to each employer by the inspector of taxes before the start of the tax year in the UK. They are used with the employee's tax code number to calculate the amount of income tax due to be paid with each wage payment (PAYE). The tables, which are in two parts (A and B), have a page for each week of the tax year. Table A shows the weekly and monthly free pay for each tax code. Table B (tax due) shows the total tax due on the taxable pay to date.

Tax Year This runs from 6 April in one calendar year to 5 April in the next, and is the period over which income is assessed for tax purposes.

Technical Barriers The obstacles to trade between EC Member States caused by differences in standards and legal requirements governing aspects such as safety and quality.

Telecom Gold The British Telecom electronic mail system.

Telecommunications The transmission of information by radio waves.

Teleconferencing (See Telephone)

Telegraphic Transfer A method of making international payments between banks through the Telex service or using facsimile transmission facilities.

Telephone An electrical device for transmitting speech, consisting of a microphone and a receiver mounted on a handset. There is a worldwide system of telephone communications. A wide range of telephone services exist in the UK and the following is a summary of some of the important ones:

- **Advice of duration and charge call (ADC)** – call connected and timed by operator. Caller is advised cost of call by operator when call is terminated.
- **Alarm call** – the subscriber arranges for the exchange to ring a specified telephone number at a particular time.
- **Call card** – cards which can be bought in the Post Office and some other shops and used in special public call boxes. The value of the card is reduced as call time is used up. They are a useful alternative to coins.
- **Freefone** – operator-connected calls on a transferred charge basis. They are used by businesses which wish to allow people to make telephone calls to them without payment, thus encouraging custom.
- **Personal calls (person to person)** – a telephone operator connects caller with a particular person. Charge does not begin until the requested person is obtained. The cost is the normal operator-connected charge plus a basic nominal fee.
- **Radiophone** – telephone contact to and from moving vehicles.
- **Teleconferencing** – a service which allows more people to be linked by telephone.
- **Telephone credit card** – a card which allows the holder to make

operator-connected calls and charge costs to their normal telephone bill.

- **Transferred charge call** – operator-connected call where the receiver of the call accepts the charge.

Telephone Answering Machine An apparatus connected to the telephone to record messages when the telephone is unattended.

Telephone Credit Card Allows the holder to make operator-connected calls and charge the cost to their normal telephone bill.

Telemessage A telecommunication correspondence service in the UK operated through British Telecom and the Post Office. Telemessages can be sent by telephone or Telex up to 10.00 p.m. daily (7.00 p.m. Sundays and Bank Holidays) for delivery by post throughout the UK and some overseas countries. Access to the service is obtained through the main telephone operator who connects the caller with the Telemessage service and the message is dictated to the operator. In the UK Telemessages are presented on A4-sized headed paper and delivered with the next day's first class post in a distinctive Telemessage envelope. A standard message (each containing the same text) can be sent to several addresses at a lower price. An extension to this service allows a business to store names and addresses of people it communicates with regularly on a Telemessage service central computer. These names and addresses can be retrieved for quick handling when a sender wishes to send a common text to many addresses.

Telephone Alphabet An alphabet which substitutes names for letters when spelling out important words. One of the limitations of the telephone is that because the message is not in visual form it is easy for mistakes to occur because some words, letters and numbers can sound similar on the telephone. For example, seven can sound like eleven, S sounds like F, especially if the person speaking is not very clear.

Telephone alphabet		
A Alfred	J Jack	S Samuel
B Benjamin	K King	T Tommy
C Charlie	L London	U Uncle
D David	M Mary	V Victor
E Edward	N Nellie	W William
F Frederick	O Oliver	X X-ray
G George	P Peter	Y Yellow
H Harry	Q Queen	Z Zebra
I Isaac	R Robert	

Teleprinter   A telegraphic apparatus consisting of a keyboard transmitter and visual display unit. Data typed into keyboard is converted into coded pulses for transmission to other similar devices on other sites, or other parts of the world. The receiving terminal converts the incoming signals and prints out the message.

Teletex   Typed messages can be prepared in the normal fashion on a special electronic typewriter terminal. The prepared text can be automatically transmitted in seconds, over ordinary telephone lines, to a receiving terminal where it is printed out or displayed on a screen in exactly the same format as the original. Teletex is in fact an improved, higher quality telex service.

Teletext   (See CEEFAX)

Telex   A communication system whereby a message can be sent from one teleprinter to another teleprinter in any part of the world. (See Teleprinter)

Teller   A bank clerk who receives and pays out money at the bank counter.

Tenant   Someone who holds property and pays rent.

Tender   1) An offer, usually in writing, to supply goods or services at a fixed price   2) An offer to purchase securities at a stated price   3) An offer of payment of a debt.

Term Bill   A bill of exchange which is payable at the end of a period after acceptance, i.e. 90 days.

Terminal   A piece of electronic equipment which provides access to information contained on file in a computer. It also provides a means of data input as well as output.

Terminal Trading   (See Futures Trading)

Term Shares   A type of share available through a building society where money is deposited for a fixed period of years and the investor receives an enhanced rate of interest.

Terms of Payment   When goods are purchased the seller will indicate the method of payment required, for example, cash with order, payment within 28 days, etc.

Territorial Waters   An area of the offshore coast and sea over which a State exercises its rights, control and sovereignty.

Tertiary Production   The final stage of the production process in which services are provided. These may be direct services, for example, hairdressing, where the consumer obtains satisfaction from the service itself, or they may be indirect services, for example, retailing, where the consumer obtains satisfaction not from the service but from the product that the service has helped to reach the consumer.

Testcheck   An accounting method of verifying selected items in an account for the purpose of determining the correctness of the entire account; a form of sampling.

Test House   A commercial organisation which provides facilities for manufacturers, trading standards officers and others wishing to check the compliance of a product with EC standards and regulations.

Testimonial   A recommendation of the character, ability, etc., of a person or of a consumer product or service, especially by a person whose opinion is valued.

Test Marketing   A limited launch of a new product or service in a particular area, or for a short period of time, in order to assess potential demand prior to embarking on full-scale production or supply.

Thermie   The EC programme on new and renewable sources of energy.

Third Country   A term used by EC Member States to refer to any country outside the EC. The term should not be confused with Third World, or less-developed countries.

Third Party   Someone not directly connected with another but who is affected by that other person's action. For example, in the case of insurance the third party would be someone who has been injured or whose property has been damaged. The first and second parties are the insured and the insurance company.

Third Party Insurance   A type of motor insurance which only covers risks to third parties.

Third Party, Fire and Theft Insurance   A type of motor insurance which only covers the risks to third parties and to the vehicle occurring from fire or theft.

Third World   Less-developed countries. The poorer countries of the world, such as Ethiopia and India. Third world countries are 'less-developed' than the rich industrialised countries such as Japan and the USA.

Threshold Price The minimum prices at which agricultural produce from non-EC countries can come into the Community. Threshold prices take account of internal distribution costs to ensure that 'target prices' cannot be undercut.

Tied Premises that are owned by a particular business that mainly sells the products of that company, for example, a garage owned by a particular oil company, or a public house owned by a brewery.

Time and Motion Study The detailed analysis of industrial or working procedures in order to determine the most efficient methods of operation.

Time Charter A contract for the hire of a ship or a vehicle for a certain period of time.

Tip A voluntary payment given for services in excess of the standard charge. Sometimes referred to as a gratuity.

TIR Transports Internationaux Routiers (French: International Road Transport). A permit which allows sealed vehicles or containers which have been inspected and sealed by Customs to pass across EC frontiers with the minimum of further checks.

Title A right to ownership of property.

Title Deed A deed which shows a right to property.

Token Coin A coin which has a higher value for exchange purposes than the metal it contains. Most coins in circulation today are token coins, but this was not always the case in the past.

Top Up A principle lender such as a building society may feel unable to provide all the finance requested. The remainder, a top up, is provided by another institution, say, an insurance company.

Tort A wrong, not arising out of contract, which gives rise to an action at law.

Total Allowable Catch (TAC) Total amount of fish which can be caught in EC waters in any one year. TAC is decided under the Common Fisheries Policy. The overall TAC includes different amounts for different types of fish.

Total Loss   An insurance term which refers to a complete loss, for example, the loss of both a ship and its cargo.

Tourism   The business of tourist travel and the services connected with it.

Trade   The act of buying and selling goods or services.

Trade Associations   National organisations representing particular sectors, such as retailers or manufacturers of a particular product. These associations form Codes of Practice which member companies are expected to honour. National trade associations often form European 'umbrella' federations. Some examples of UK trade associations are the Association of British Travel Agents (ABTA) and the Motor Agents Association (MAA).

Trade Credit   The situation where a seller of goods allows a buyer to have the goods immediately and pay for them later.

Trade Cycle   The recurrent fluctuation between boom and recession in the economic activity of a country. Sometimes referred to as the business cycle.

- **Boom** – period of high economic growth
- **Recession** – a period of high unemployment and low economic growth
- **Slump** – a sudden and severe fall in economic activity
- **Recovery** – increased economic activity and movement towards higher levels.

Trade Discount   A reduction that is allowed off a list price to certain customers (for example, other traders) to enable them to make a profit on the resale of goods purchased.

Traded Option   An agreement giving the right to buy or sell at stated prices within a given period. The option can be bought or sold during the option period and exercised by the holder at the end of the period.

Trade Fair   An exhibition of products or services, generally at a large centre, and particularly aimed at attracting traders and others with specialist interest. The department of Trade and Industry plays an important part in promoting UK products and services at overseas trade fairs.

Trade Gap   The amount by which the value of a country's visible imports exceeds that of visible exports; an unfavourable balance of trade.

Trade-In   A used article given in part payment for the purchase of a replacement article.

Trade Journal   A periodical containing new developments, discussions, etc., concerning a particular trade or profession.

Trade Mark   The name or symbol used to identify the goods produced by a particular manufacturer or distributed by a particular dealer and to distinguish them from products associated with competing manufacturers or suppliers. It is officially registered and legally protected.

Trade Name   The name under which a commercial enterprise operates in business.

Trade-Off   Where a concession is granted by one party to another in exchange for another concession or benefit.

Trade Price   The preferential price at which a trader will sell to others in the same line of business.

Trades Description Acts 1968 and 1972   An Act of the UK Parliament which makes it an offence punishable by fine or imprisonment to falsely describe goods or services offered for sale. The Act applies to verbal or written descriptions.

Trade Union   An association of employees formed to improve their incomes and working conditions by collective bargaining with the employer or employer organisation. There is a legal requirement that all members must be registered.

Trading Account   A financial statement which shows all the inflows and outflows of a firm's money within a period of time.

Trading Certificate   The Certificate issued by the Registrar of Companies authorising a company to begin trading.

Trading Estate   An area set aside especially for trading firms with industrial units and warehouses and good links with roads and other transport facilities.

Trading Stamps   Stamps offered by traders in accordance with the value of purchases and can be exchanged for cash or goods from the issuing company at a later date. It is seen as a sort of bonus for the purchaser and is used to stimulate sales.

Trading Standards Office An office run by local authorities to provide advice and assistance and to follow up complaints by consumers, such as those related to faulty goods or services. Informative literature provided by the Office of Fair Trading is also available at these offices.

Trades Union Congress (TUC) The major association of UK trade unions, which includes all the larger unions.

Tramp Ships Independent ships not attached to shipping conferences and without a regular timetable. They are hired or chartered for a particular voyage or period of time to go wherever required.

Transaction The complete process of a business deal including order and supply. A cash transaction is one where payment is made immediately, and a credit transaction is where payment is made at some later date.

Transfer Charge (See Telephone)

Transfer Deed A legal document transferring property from one person to another.

Transhipment To transfer cargo or packages from one transport to another, for example, from ship to ship, rail to road, etc.

Transit The passage of goods or people, for example, goods 'in transit' are on the journey towards their destination.

Transportation System The means through which goods and people are moved from one place to another.

Transport Documents Documents which show that goods have been despatched, for example, shipping documentation.

Traveller's Cheques Special cheques which are charged against a bank and, therefore, guaranteed by the bank. This makes them acceptable throughout the world and useful to the business person or the individual when travelling. They can be purchased at the local bank, and other forms of financial institution such as a building society, for use abroad to obtain foreign currency. The cheques are 'safe' because if they are lost or stolen they can immediately be cancelled and the bank will replace them. A further safeguard requires those encashing the cheques to sign them in front of the cashier having first produced proof of identity (for example, passport).

Travelling Auditor A staff auditor employed by a firm who examines the books of account at branches and other outlying points for the head office.

Treasurer   The person who has the responsibility for the financial aspects of an organisation.

Treasury   The central State department which manages the financial resources of the UK and controls public expenditure. The government minister and member of the Cabinet responsible for the Treasury is the Chancellor of the Exchequer.

Treasury Bills   A government security issued weekly. They are in fact a promissory note; a promise to pay a stated sum within a given period not exceeding one year, although normally the period is 91 days after issue. They are an important form of short-term borrowing for the Government. Treasury Bills are bought almost entirely by the 'discount houses', which put in weekly tenders for the Bills,

Treaty of Rome 1957   A treaty signed on 25 March 1957 by Belgium, Luxembourg, The Netherlands, France, West Germany and Italy, which set up the European Economic Community. The UK became a member in 1972.

Trust   Money or property held by appointed persons, called trustees, for the benefit of others to be used for defined purposes.

Trustee   A person to whom the legal title to property is entrusted to hold or use for another's benefit.

Trustee in Bankruptcy   A person appointed by a Court to take charge and manage a bankrupt's affairs.

Turn   The difference between the buying and selling price of something, for example, foreign currency, shares, etc.

Turn-Around Time   The time taken for a ship to enter a port, unload its cargo, load a new cargo and leave the port.

Turnover   A term used to refer to the gross income or sales of an organisation over the previous year. Turnover can indicate how 'active' the firm has been in a given period. Generally speaking, the greater the turnover the more business the firm is doing, although this is not always the case.

Turnover, Net   A figure which is obtained by taking the total sales of the business minus the value of goods returned or credit notes issued.

Turnover, Rate of The number of times the average stock of the business has been sold in the year. There are two methods of calculating the rate of stock turnover depending whether the stock is looked at in terms of cost price or selling price.

1) $\text{Rate of turnover} = \dfrac{\text{cost of stock sold}}{\text{average stock at cost price}}$

2) $\text{Rate of turnover} = \dfrac{\text{net turnover}}{\text{average stock at selling price}}$

(Average stock is worked out by taking the stock value at the beginning and at the end of the trading period, adding them, and dividing by two)

Tycoon A highly successful business person who has amassed a large personal fortune.

Type Approval A car sold in the UK has to conform to UK rules, such as MOT test regulations. Such rules, known as type approval, may differ between EC Member States and constitute to barriers to trade. The European Commission has proposed EC-wide type approval regulations to overcome this.

Uberrimae Fidei The Latin for 'of the utmost good faith'. The contract between the insurer and the customer differs from a normal contract in that it is a contract of 'the utmost good faith'. This means that both the insurance company and the customer must act with 'utmost good faith'. Both must reveal all material facts relevant to the contract being arranged. Obviously, since it is the customer that is seeking insurance cover, the main responsibility of utmost good faith lies with them.

Ultra Vires A Latin phrase which means beyond the legal power or authority of a person, corporation, agent, etc.

UK Insurance Market The centre of the UK insurance market is based in the Lloyd's Corporation (Lloyds of London).

Under Bond Imported goods which are temporarily stored in a bonded warehouse awaiting re-exporting.

Under-Insurance The buying of insurance to cover a value lower than the actual value of an item insured.

Underwriter A person who provides a guarantee, for a fee, against risks, for example, when new shares are issued the underwriter will guarantee that all shares will be sold by buying up any shares that have not been bought. Similarly, an insurance underwriter will guarantee to indemnify insurance claims made against them.

Undischarged Bankrupt   A person who has been declared bankrupt by a court and has not been discharged. When discharged, the slate is wiped clean, which means that all outstanding debts have been paid or written off. An undischarged bankrupt cannot:

- Be a company director
- Manage a company, directly or indirectly
- Be an MP, a JP, or a local councillor
- Operate a business in a name other than that in which they were declared bankrupt. In addition the undischarged bankrupt has certain limitations in respect of the use of a bank account and access to credit facilities.

Unearned Income   The income obtained from investments as opposed to income received as earnings from employment.

Unemployment   A term applied to those people seeking employment who are capable of, and available for work.

- Cyclical unemployment is caused by a lack of demand for goods and services in the economy.
- Frictional unemployment is of short duration and is caused as workers move from one job to another.
- Seasonal unemployment is caused by changes in demand for workers at different times of the year.
- Structural unemployment is caused by insufficient capital (for example, machinery, factories, etc.,) in the economy.

Unfair Dismissal   When someone has been unfairly given notice of discharge from their employment.

Unit Price   A price for foodstuffs, etc., stated or shown as the cost per unit, as per pound, per kilogram, etc.

Unit Trust   An investment trust that issues units or a part of the investment for public sale, the holders of which are creditors and not shareholders. The money received from investors is used (by the trustees/managers) to buy shares in a variety of companies, thus reducing the risk of loss.

Unladen Weight   The weight of a vehicle without its load.

Unlimited Liability   The legal obligation of the owners of an unlimited liability organisation to pay all the debts of the business, even to the extent of giving up their own personal wealth. Usually such firms are small and their liability in the event of bankruptcy tends not to be large. Sole traders and partnerships are examples of businesses that have unlimited liability. (Compare with Limited Liability)

Unofficial Dispute/Strike   A labour dispute that has not been accepted as 'official' by the trade union whose members are in dispute.

Unsecured Creditor   A creditor owed money by a debtor and who relies entirely on the debtor's promise to repay the amount outstanding, in other words the debt is not secured against some asset.

Unsolicited Goods and Services Act 1971   An Act of the UK Parliament which makes it illegal to demand payment for goods or services that have not been ordered. Should unsolicited goods be delivered, the consumer has two clear courses of action:

1) They can write to the firm giving their name and address from where the goods can be collected. If the trader fails to collect the goods within 30 days they belong to the holder.
2) Alternatively, if unsolicited goods are not collected by the trader within six months they become the property of the holder.

User Friendly   A term used in relation to computer software which is easy to use.

Unsocial Hours   Hours of work falling outside the 'normal' working day.

Utility   The usefulness or satisfaction obtained from an article or service. Some economists argue that as the number of units of a product consumed increases, the utility or satisfaction declines. If one takes the simple example of chocolate bars it is easy to see how this is the case, but with other more complex examples it is less easy to see.

Utmost Good Faith   (See Uberrimae Fidei)

Value Added Tax (VAT)   The most important indirect tax in the UK because it is the main general expenditure tax levied by central government. It is a tax imposed on the value added to goods and services at every stage of production. When several traders are involved in the movement of goods from the producer to the consumer, each will charge VAT to the person to whom they sell. Each trader, however, only pays to Customs and Excise the amount of VAT they have charged their customers less the amount of tax paid to their suppliers. In this way it can be seen that each trader pays VAT on the difference between how much the product was sold for and what was paid for it. This difference is called 'value added'. Therefore, tax is paid on the value that has been added to the product, and this is how this tax gets its name. The rate of VAT is decided by the government. Some goods and services do not have VAT charged on them because they are either rated or exempt.

- Zero rated goods are those subject to VAT, but the rate of VAT is 0 per cent. The trader who sells zero VAT rated goods may reclaim the VAT they have paid to their suppliers from the Customs and Excise Department.
- Exempt goods are those not subject to any VAT. The trader who selling goods that are exempt may not reclaim any VAT they have paid.

Variable Costs   Costs which change according to the amount of business done or the number of goods produced, for example, expenditure on raw materials, fuel, lighting and the wages of those directly involved in production. These costs are higher at higher levels of output. (See also Fixed Costs)

Variety Chain Stores   A chain store which sells a varied range of domestic products, for example, Woolworths. (See also Chain Store)

Vending Machine   A machine that automatically dispenses consumer goods such as cigarettes, confectionery, food and petrol, when money is inserted.

Vendor   The seller.

Venture Capital   Money loaned to new and untested businesses.

Vertical Intergration/ Vertical Merger   A situation where two companies dealing with different stages of production and supply join together. Vertical integration may be either backwards or forwards:

- Backwards integration could be where a firm merges with its supplier. For example, a food manufacturer may join with some farms to ensure control over its supplies.
- Forwards integration can be seen where a manufacturer merges with a

retail chain in order to ensure an outlet for their products. (See also Horizontal Integration)

VDU (See Visual Display Unit)

Video Conferencing (See Confravision)

Viewdata System A two-way information system which gives the user access to information held on computers. The system contains a variety of information for business and domestic users, such as share and commodity prices, exchange rates, and interest rates. The British Telecom Prestel service is an example of a viewdata system.

Visible Trade The total import and export of things that can be seen (goods) within a given period of time.

Visual Display Unit (VDU) Screen similar to that of a television set that is used to display the output of a computer.

Vocation A specified occupation or profession.

Voluntary Codes Codes which are established by trade associations to set a standard of business practice to be honoured by all members of the industry.

Voluntary Export Restraint (VER) The ultimatum given to non-EC countries when they are too successful in exporting goods into the EC to voluntarily reduce their exports or face imposed tariffs or import quotas.

Voyage Charter (See Charter Party)

Wages Payment in return for work or services. (See also Differential)

Wages Council A body set up by the government for the establishment of minimum wages and conditions in forms of employment where union representation is considered to be weak.

Walkout Withdrawal of labour by employees leaving the premises. A strike.

Wall Street The main financial centre of New York where the principal US banks and the US Stock Exchange are sited.

Warehousing A commercial activity which assists trade by providing bulk storage facilities for goods until they are required. (See also Bonded)

Warehouse　A large building used for storage. It is essential that such a building should not only be secure but also be able to maintain goods in the right condition, for example, frozen, fresh, dry, etc. A 'bonded' warehouse is one that is owned by a business but supervised by HM Customs and Excise Department officers. They are used to store imported goods which are subject to duties until they are paid, or the goods are re-exported.

Warranty　A guarantee given for a fixed period by a manufacturer to a buyer that a defective product will be repaired or replaced free of charge.

Weights and Measures Act 1963　An Act of the UK Parliament which aims to protect consumers.

- It requires the quantity of pre-packed goods to be shown on the container.
- It makes short weight or short measurement an offence.
- It requires certain goods to be sold in 'prescribed quantities' (for example, milk is sold in pints).

WHICH　The monthly magazine of the Consumers' Association in which is published the results of tests and investigations into goods and services, comparison of products and recommendations of 'best buys'.

Whispering Campaign　A word of mouth or 'whispering campaign' is a subtle and effective form of advertising where the advertiser tries to encourage people to recommend their products to others, for example, by giving them free samples.

White Collar Union　A union of office or other non-manual workers.

Whole Life Policy　A type of life assurance policy where the policy-holder pays regular premiums throughout their life, no matter how long they live, and when they die the insurance company pays the sum assured to their relatives or a named person. By contrast a 'term' policy involves payment of premiums for a set period. If the person dies during the period the sum assured is paid, but if they live to the end of the period no payment is made.

Wholesale Market　Products that perish quickly, such as fruit and vegetables, fish and meat, are often sold through wholesale markets. Retailers and wholesalers meet at these markets very early in the morning to trade. Examples of these markets in London are New Covent Garden (fruit and vegetables) and Smithfield (meat).

Wholesaler A trader who deals with manufacturers, retailers and other wholesalers, but not with consumers. The wholesaler provides services for both the producer and the retailer. For the producer the wholesaler:

- Reduces transport costs
- Advises producer of current trends
- Finishes goods by grading, packing and branding
- Makes mass production possible by ordering in large quantities and therefore reducing production costs.

For the retailer the wholesaler:

- Offers choice of products from many producers
- Supplies small quantities to suit retailers' needs
- Advises latest trends and 'best buys'
- Locally situated providing quick access to goods
- Pre-packs goods ready for retailers' shelves.

Wholesale Price The price at which a wholesaler sells his goods to a retailer.

Wildcat An unofficial strike where workers stop work without union backing. (See also Unofficial Strike)

Windfall An unexpected gain or profit.

Winding-Up The process of closing down a company either voluntarily or upon the instructions of a Court. It is sometimes referred to as 'going into liquidation'.

Window Shopping Looking at goods on display in shops but not necessarily purchasing, although comparison of prices may be made.

With Profits A life assurance policy that pays a sum of money to the policyholder at the end of the period covered by a term assurance.

World Bank The International Bank for Reconstruction and Development (IBRD). The World Bank's capital comes from subscriptions from the rich countries, from bonds issued in world financial markets, and from the Bank's trading activities. The function of the Bank is to assist the reconstruction and development of member countries by providing capital for investment.

Wordprocessor A computer which can store, correct, and read written information.

Worker Co-operative A business that is owned and controlled by its own workforce.

Worker Director An employee of a limited company who is appointed to the board of directors.

Worker Participation The involvement of workers (usually through representatives) in discussions as part of the decision-making process of a business. (See also Works Council)

Working Capital Capital that is continually changing in quantity, total value or nature. Examples: stocks, cash,bank balance, and the amount of money owed to a firm by its customers (debtors). Working capital can be calculated by:

current assets − current liabilities = working capital

Working Capital Ratio A measure of a firm's ability to meet short-term liabilities. It is calculated as follows:

$$\frac{\text{current assets}}{\text{current liabilities}} = \text{working capital ratio}$$

Working Party A group established to investigate a specific issue.

Works Council A formal group consisting of both management and worker representative which meet to discuss and seek solutions to mutual problems relating to the organisation.

Work Study The process of making a detailed study of work with a view to achieving improved productivity.

Work to Rule A form of restrictive practice. Workers follow the rules and regulations of the company exactly. By sticking strictly to the rules in this way work is slowed down and productivity is reduced.

Working Population All those persons between the school-leaving age and the retirement age who are available for work.

World Intellectual Property Organisation An international organisation, based in Geneva, to deal with worldwide copyright trademarks and patents.

World Prices A term used by EC Member States to refer to those prices at which agricultural produce is sold outside the EC. World prices are usually below those of the EC, which are propped up by the Common Agricultural Policy. The world price is in effect the EC price less the export refund.

Writ   A document issued in the name of the Crown or a court, commanding the person to whom it is addressed to do or to refrain from doing some specified act.

Wrongful Dismissal   (See Unfair Dismissal)

Xerography   A photocopying process in which an electrostatic image is formed on a plate or cylinder. The plate or cylinder is dusted with a resinous powder which adheres to the charged regions, and the image is then transferred to a sheet of paper on which it is fixed by heating.

Yield   The real annual return on an investment, for example, the interest or dividend of a debenture or share, divided by its market price.

$$\frac{\text{Dividend}}{\text{Market value}} = \text{Yield} \qquad \frac{90p}{£2} = 4.5\% \text{ Yield}$$

Zero-Rated (VAT)   Zero-rated goods are those on which no Value Added Tax is charged.

Zip Code   (See Post Code)